The
ORVIS
Fly Pattern Index

by John R. Harder

A PLUME BOOK

PLUME
Published by the Penguin Group
Penguin Books USA Inc., 375 Hudson Street, New York, New York
10014, U.S.A.
Penguin Books Ltd, 27 Wrights Lane, London W8 5TZ, England
Penguin Books Australia Ltd, Ringwood, Victoria, Australia
Penguin Books Canada Ltd, 10 Alcorn Ave., Toronto, Ontario,
Canada M4V 3B2
Penguin Books (N.Z.) Ltd, 182-190 Wairau Road, Auckland 10, New
Zealand

Penguin Books Ltd, Registered Offices: Harmondsworth, Middlesex,
England

Published by Plume, an imprint of New American Library, a division of
Penguin Books USA Inc.

Index of Orvis Fly Patterns, Volume 1A first published in 1978 by
   The Orvis Company,
Index of Orvis Fly Patterns, Volume 2A published in 1980
First published in one volume in 1990 by The Stephen Greene Press/
   Pelham Books
   Distributed by Viking Penguin, a division of Penguin Books USA Inc.

10 9 8 7 6 5

Acknowledgments
Color photography - William Cheney
Black/white photography - Richard Disque

 REGISTERED TRADEMARK—MARCA REGISTRADA

Library of Congress Cataloging in Publication Data
Harder, John R.
   Orvis Fly Pattern Index.
   1. Fly tying.   2. Flies, Artificial.   I. Title.
SH451.H27 1990   688.7'912   89-23763

Printed in The United States of America

CONTENTS

FOREWORD

Through the years, we at Orvis have received numerous phone calls and letters requesting pattern descriptions to tie the standard Orvis Flies. Our customers have frequently commented that they use the Orvis Catalog pictures as a pattern guide. These phone calls, letters and comments prompted the publishing of "The Orvis Fly Pattern Index."

The "Index" is not intended to be a comprehensive book of tying techniques as the market is well stocked with publications of that sort. Rather, it is intended to be a visual reference and pattern guide for tying popular and classic Orvis Fly Patterns.

It does include Basic Tying Instructions and several pages of step-by-step tying instructions, pictures and comments to help with the more complex patterns not commonly included in most fly tying publications.

We hope you will have many enjoyable hours tying and fishing the flies illustrated in "The Orvis Fly Pattern Index."

DEDICATION

To the Orvis Fly Tyers
who tied many of the flies pictured
and, through their dedication to fly tying,
have set the standard
for commercially tied flies.

ACKNOWLEDGMENTS

I would like to thank the many fly tyers for contributing their fly patterns to this volume and to the sport of fly fishing, and also to those fly tyers, whose identity has been lost with the passing of time. I would also like to thank Tom Rosenbauer for writing the fly tying section, "Eleven Basic Flies That Will Teach You To Tie".

PART I

Eleven
Basic Flies
That Will Teach
You To Tie

Eleven Basic Flies That Will Teach You to Tie

The following eleven flies will give you a basic education in fly tying, and will teach you techniques that can be used on thousands of patterns. Unlike many of the basic fly tying instructions you'll read, they include up-to-date flies that are popular today, like the Woolly Bugger and Parachute Hare's Ear dry and the Crazy Charlie bonefish fly.

If you're just beginning, we suggest that you start with the first fly we've listed and tie the flies the order they appear. Tie at least six flies of a single pattern before moving on, so you'll develop the techniques you'll use on successive patterns. All good fly tiers work this way for efficiency, setting up for one pattern at a time. Your sixth fly will look a lot better than your first — but they'll all catch fish. The patterns and their sequence have been especially selected for the techniques they illustrate.

As you tie these patterns and learn new techniques, one of the most important considerations is proportion. Good proportions aren't just stylistic considerations for fly tiers. Everything a game fish eats is symmetrical, so a well-tied fly imitates the natural proportions and symmetry of insects, crustaceans, and bait fish. Where possible, we've listed both a length in inches for wings and tails — and more importantly, their relation to the hook shank and the gape of the hook. Most fly proportions are based on these two measurements, and they give you an instant yardstick as you're tying.

Glossary

Here are a few terms not explained in the text that might make your tying easier.

Back — When referring to directions on a fly, you wind **back** toward the bend of the hook — to the left for right handed tiers.

Barb — The part of a hook that holds the hook in a fish's mouth, just behind the point.

Bend — The point where the shank of the hook begins to turn down.

Butt — When referring to feathers or hairs, the heavier end. The butt end is usually snipped off or tied under when constructing a fly.

Eye — The circular piece of wire at the front of a fly to which you attach your tippet.

Fiber — A single strand of feather or hackle.

Flaring — Constricting a bunch of hair against a hook so it sticks out in all directions.

Forward — Moving from the bend of the hook to the eye, for right-hand tiers it's moving from left to right.

Gape — The vertical distance between the point of the hook and the shank, used for measuring correct proportions.

Point — The sharp end of a hook that first penetrates the fish's mouth.

Quill — The center stem of a feather to which the fibers are attached.

Shank — The long straight portion of a hook, measured from the eye to the beginning of the bend. Used to obtain correct proportions.

Tip — The finer end of a feather or hair, usually tapered to a fine point.

Web — The portion of a feather that is dull-colored and downy, usually at the bottom center of the quill on a hackle fiber (but some hackles notably hen hackles, have *all* webby fibers).

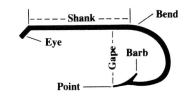

Hook Cross Reference Chart

	Orvis	Tiemco	Mustad	VMC
1X Fine Dry Fly TD Eye, Wide Gape Bronze	1509	100	—	—
1X Fine Dry Fly Straight Eye, Wide Gape Bronze	1637	101	94859	—
1X Fine Dry Fly TD Eye, Wide Gape Black	1635	1024	—	—
1X Fine Dry Fly TD Eye, Perfect Bend Bronze	1523	5210	94840	9280
2XL, 1X Fine Dry Fly TD Eye, Perfect Bend Bronze	1638	5212	94831	—
2XL, Humped Shank TD Eye Hoppers and Terrestrials Bronze	1640	1640	9671 Bent	9279 Bent
2X Wide, 2X Short TD Eye, Fine Wire Bronze - Shrimp/Pupae	1639	2487	—	—
2X Heavy - Wet/Nymph TD Eye, Sproat Bend Bronze	1641	3769	3906	8526
2X Heavy, 1X Long Wet/Nymph - TD Eye Sproat Bend - Bronze	1642	3761	3906B	8527
2X Long, Nymph TD Eye, Perfect Bend Bronze	1524	5262	9671	9279
3X Long, Nymph TD Eye, Perfect Bend Bronze	1526	5263	9672	—
3X Long, Nymph Straight Eye, Special Bend Bronze	1510	200	—	—

Hook Cross Reference Chart *(continued)*

	Orvis	Tiemco	Mustad	VMC
4X Long, Streamer TD Eye, Perfect Bend Bronze	1511	300	79580	9283
Swimming Nymph Straight Eye, Special Bend Bronze	1512	400	—	—
Salmon Dry TU Loop Eye Fine Wire - Black	1644	7989	90240	—
Salmon Wet TU Loop Eye Heavy Wire - Black	1645	7999	36890	—
Saltwater - Stainless Steel Straight Eye O'Shaughnessy Bend	0549	—	34007	—
Egg Hook - 3X Short Straight Eye - Heavy Wire Perfect Bend - Bronze	0595	—	9174	—
Bass Bug (Stinger) Straight Eye Special Wide Gape Bronze	0520	—	37187 *or* 37189	—

Starting Your Thread

Hold the thread at a 45° angle to the shank of the hook on the side of the hook facing you, with the bobbin at the top in your right hand and the loose end of the thread in the thumb and forefinger of your left hand underneath the hook.

Holding your left hand steady, bring the bobbin around the back of the hook, underneath, and then as you come around the near side of the hook, push it to the left while pushing your left hand slightly to the right.

Now just use the bobbin to continue winding to the left, over the loose end of the thread. After five turns, trim the loose end close to the hook and begin tying your pattern.

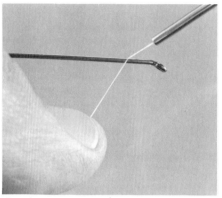

Step 1.

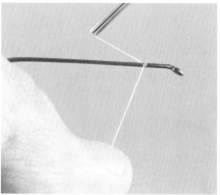

Step 2.

The Pinch Method

Many things like tinsel and dry fly hackles can be merely placed next to the shank and wound over with thread. Bunches of hair or feathers, however, need to be attached in a manner that keeps them from rolling around the hook. For this you use the pinch method.

Over a base of thread (never over a bare hook unless you intentionally want the material to roll around the hook, as when you spin deer hair), hold the material in place with the tips of your thumb and forefinger pinched over the spot where the thread will attach the material to the hook. Bring the thread in a loose loop over the top of the material, at the same time rocking your thumb and forefinger back onto the first knuckle so they open up slightly. After the loop is formed over the material and the bobbin is hanging below, close your fingers over the thread, the material, and the sides of the hook at the same time.

Now put the pressure on the thread by pulling straight down, until the thread is wrapped firmly around the material and the hook, and without moving anything else, open up your fingers and repeat the loop and pinch. Three or four times will usually be enough to attach anything to the hook. Before trimming anything, wind over the butt ends of the materials several times, and always hold the bunch of feathers or hair while trimming, to keep them from getting moved out of alignment.

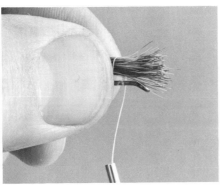

Step 1.

Step 2.

Step 3.

Whip Finishing a Head

When you finish your fly, you need to tie off the head to keep it from unraveling. A couple of half hitches are adequate but not the best way. The best method is a whip finish, which winds the thread under itself 5 or 6 times. The best way to whip finish is with a special tool, which makes it easier to get into small places and puts more tension on the winds than you can by hand.

It's best to whip finish in the center of the head, because if you whip finish near a wet fly wing or dry fly hackle, you tend to knock wings out of alignment or wind hackles under. If you whip finish too close to the eye of the hook, the whip finish may slip off the hook shank and onto the eye.

With the bobbin hanging at the spot where you want to finish the head, pull out 8'' of thread so the bobbin is hanging 8'' below the hook.

Hold the whip finish tool with your pinky, fourth finger, and third finger on the far side of the brass shaft, your thumb on the near side, and your forefinger bracing the chrome rotating part of the tool on its far side so it can't rotate. The open end of the two loops on the tool should be facing toward your right.

Place the indent at the bottom of the large loop against the thread on the side facing you. Keeping your forefinger against the

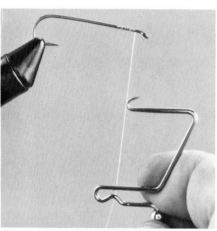

Step 1.

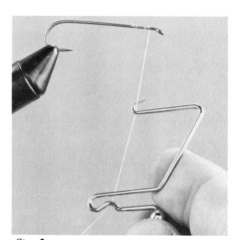

Step 2.

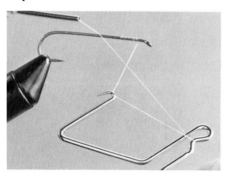

Step 3.

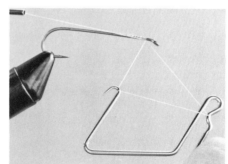

Step 4.

tool, and the thread inside the indent, bring the bobbin up over the top of the fly.

As you're bringing the bobbin over the top of the fly, catch the piece of thread farthest from you with the hook at the top of the tool. Release the tool with your forefinger (but still holding the handle). Bring the tool up over the top of the hook, at the same time bringing the bobbin back underneath the hook, crossing the thread on the near side of the hook shank.

A loop should now be formed, with the thread intersecting at the hook exactly where you want your whip finish to be.

Rotate the handle of the tool around the eye of the fly, pushing away from you on top of the hook and then back toward you on the bottom. Rotate the tool 5 times around the hook.

Rotate the handle 90° so it's now perpendicular to the shank of the hook. Move the handle of the tool to a vertical position by bringing the end closest to you up. The thread will slip out of the indent. Now pull on the bobbin to tighten the loop, and slip the hook out after the knot is tightened. Trim the thread and you're done.

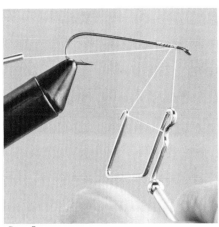

Step 5.

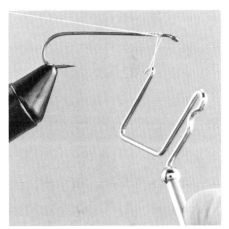

Step 6.

The Woolly Bugger

The Woolly Bugger is in a class by itself. Part nymph, part streamer, it has replaced the Muddler Minnow as the number one big trout catcher. It will also catch about any other fish that will take a fly, including bass, panfish, pike, salmon, steelhead, and even bonefish. It is very easy to tie and catches fish even when tied quite scraggly, so it's a good fly for your first attempt.

Techniques Learned: Tying in Marabou
Winding Chenille
Winding palmered hackle
Weighting a hook

Step 1: The Woolly Bugger is almost always tied weighted, usually the forward 1/3 of the hook, so the fly bobs in the water when retrieved. For the size 6 streamer hook shown here, wind about 20 turns of .021 lead wire directly from the spool as shown. Leave plenty of room near the eye of the hook, at least 3/8 inch. Break both ends of the lead wire by pulling on it and push the turns together with your thumbnails.

Step 2: Start your thread just in front of the lead wire, then wind a bump of thread in front of the wire while pushing against the rear to keep it from sliding down the hook. Spiral the thread to the rear of the lead and wind another bump. Then spiral it back and forth over the lead wire about 10 times. Apply some head cement to the lead and let dry for a real durable underbody.

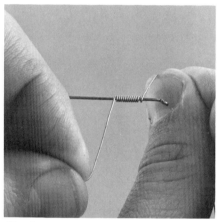

Step 1.

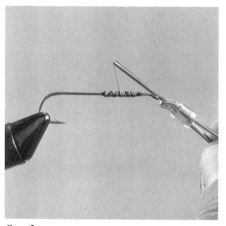

Step 2.

Step 3: Wind the thread back to the bend of the hook, just above the barb. Take a whole black marabou feather and stroke all the fibers toward the tip, into one bunch. Hold the feather against the hook and measure back from the tip a distance of one shank length, plus the distance from where the lead wire ends to the bend. Cut the feather here and moisten the butt ends with your finger tips. Lay the marabou bunch over the hook, with the butt ends just touching the turns of lead wire. Tie it in with the pinch method using three turns, then take smooth turns of thread up to the lead wire and back to the bend.

Step 4: Find a long black saddle hackle with fibers that are just slightly longer than the gape of the hook. You can measure feathers by gently flexing them around the hook — this can even be done while they're still on a saddle or strung. Grasp the hackle by the tip and stroke the fibers gently down toward the butt, leaving about 1/2 inch of the tip unstroked. Tie the tip of the hackle in with about 8 very tight turns of thread.

Step 5: Cut a 5'' piece of olive chenille for a size 6 hook off the card. With the nails of your thumb and forefinger, strip the cotton off about 1/4'' of one end of the chenille. Tie this in right on top of the saddle hackle tip with another 8 very tight turns of thread.

Step 3.

Step 4.

Step 5.

Step 6: Push the saddle hackle out of the way and wind the chenille forward, spacing each turn so it just butts up against the previous turn. To wind materials, start on top of the hook shank with your right hand, wind away from you and around the far side, then transfer the material to your right hand underneath the hook and bring it back to your left hand on top. Wind all the way past the lead, leaving *plenty* of room for a neat head (crowding the head is one of the most common problems beginners have). Tie off the chenille by holding it at a 45° angle under the hook shank with your right hand and winding straight up and down with the bobbin in your left hand. Four to six turns of thread

should secure the chenille tightly. Snip the end of the chenille very close to the hook and wind a few more turns of thread over the loose ends.

Step 7: Grasp the butt end of the saddle hackle with a pair of hackle pliers and wind forward in evenly spaced turns. This type of widely spaced hackle is called palmering. As you wind the hackle, stroke the fibers to the rear as you take each turn. Tie off where you tied in the end of the chenille and snip the end of the saddle hackle.

Step 8: Wind a neat head, whip finish, and apply a couple drops of head cement.

Step 6.

Step 7.

Step 8.

Hare's Ear Nymph

The Hare's Ear Nymph is the most popular nymph of all times. In sizes 8 through 16, it will catch trout, panfish, bass, and even salmon. It suggests a myriad of underwater life, and is best tied very fuzzy and "buggy looking." You may tie it weighted, weighting just the forward half of the hook shank, or unweighted as we're showing it here.

Techniques Learned: Hackle Fiber Tails
Dubbing a Fur Body
Tinsel Ribbing
Forming a Wing Case

Step 1: Clamp a size 10 3X long nymph hook in your vise. Start the thread at about the midpoint of the hook shank and wind back to the bend. Snip a small bunch of brown hackle fibers — about 10 or 15 — from a large neck or saddle hackle. Tie in with the pinch method, using 2 or 3 pinches. Wind forward to the midpoint of the hook shank and snip off any fibers that extend further forward.

Step 2: Cut a piece of medium oval gold tinsel, four or five inches long, and wind it under from the midpoint of the hook shank back to the bend in smooth even turns.

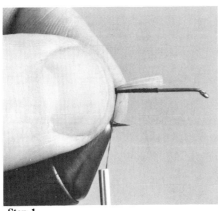

Step 1.

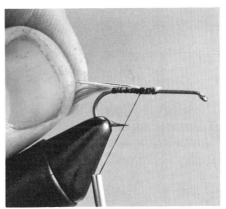

Step 2.

Step 3: For the dubbing fur you may use either a prepared hare's ear blend or make your own. To make your own, mix equal amounts of soft tan fur from the base of a pair of hare's ears with the short, dark spiky hairs clipped from the ears themselves. Put both bunches of fur together and mix by teasing the furs apart, combining them, teasing and combining until the dubbing is well mixed. To dub the fur to the thread, tease a small amount from the main ball of fur, hold it against the thread, and roll it onto the thread with a lot of pressure from your thumb and forefinger. Roll it in *one* direction only, not back and forth. (Most people use too much fur and not enough pressure). Form a slight taper, applying a little more fur as you come down the thread. Dub about 3'' of the thread for a size 10 hook, with a taper from barely covering the thread to about 1/8'' in diameter

at the point closest to the bobbin. To do this, spiral your thumb and forefinger up toward the shank as you roll dubbing onto the thread. Note: With prewaxed thread you seldom need to apply extra wax, but if you have trouble dubbing nick the thread a few times with a tube of sticky wax.

Step 4: Wind the fur-covered thread in turns that overlap about 1/2 of the previous turn. Wind only to the middle of the hook — if you have too much fur, pull it off; if you don't have enough dub a little more.

Step 5: Wind the oval tinsel forward in evenly-spaced turns . . . usually 4 or 5 turns for a size 10 hook. Tie off the tinsel under the hook with a half dozen tight turns and snip the end . . . if the end still protrudes after you snip it, cover it with a few more turns of thread.

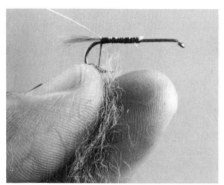

Step 3.

Step 4.

Step 5.

Step 6: Snip a 3/8'' wide piece of feather from a large gray duck or goose quill. Notice the shiny ''blood line'' at the bottom of the feather, and also that the entire feather has a shiny side and a dull side. Lay the feather on top of the hook with the uncut end facing toward the tails of the fly, shiny side up. Bring a loose turn of thread over the feather, come around the bottom of the hook, and tighten with an *upward* pull of the thread. Repeat 3 or 4 times. The upward pull will help to keep the feather from rolling off the top of the hook. Be careful not to tie in the blood line area of the feather — it should be to the right of your tie-in point. Snip the butt end of the feather 1/8'' from the eye of the fly and wind back and forth over it to keep it in place. Return the thread to the tie-in point.

Step 7: Dub about 2'' of hare's ear fur onto the thread, twice as thick as the abdomen and without any taper. Wind forward to 1/8'' behind the eye.

Step 8: Pull the wing case over the top of the thorax and tie off with upward pulls as you did when tying it in. Snip the ends of the wing case, form a neat head, whip finish, and apply head cement. A little head cement on the wing case will make it more durable, and many people tease the thorax dubbing out with a dubbing needle to simulate the legs of a nymph.

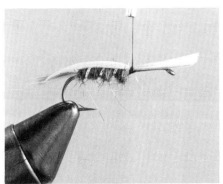

Step 6.

Step 7.

Step 8.

Eleven Basic Flies that Will Teach You to Tie   15

Blue-Wing Olive Dry

The Blue-Wing Olive is usually tied as a wingless dry fly. It imitates many different species of adult mayflies throughout the world, and is most often tied in sizes 14 through 22. Because of its simplicity, it is a great dry fly for your first attempt.

Techniques Learned: Dry Fly Tails
Dubbing a thin fur body
Selecting dry fly hackles
Winding dry fly hackles

Step 1: Start your olive 6/0 prewaxed thread on the shank of the hook, about in the middle of the shank. Wind back to the bend of the hook, just above the point. From a blue dun hackle cape, find one of the short, wide feathers at either side of the cape, about in the middle of the cape. To get some good, stiff tail fibers, find a feather that has very little web in the center and long, glossy fibers. Hold the tip of the feather between the index and third finger of one hand, and the bottom of the feather with the thumb and fourth finger. With your other hand, grasp

15-20 fibers, pull them away from the stem until the tips are all aligned and the fibers are 90° from the stem. While holding the top and bottom of the feather tightly between your fingers, pluck the fibers from the stem with a quick pull from the thumb and forefinger of your other hand. You should be left holding a nice evenly aligned bunch of tail fibers.

Step 2: Snip the webby ends of the tail fibers — this will keep them aligned better as you're tying them in. Hold the fibers over the top of the hook shank to measure them, and hold them so that the untrimmed ends are tucked in between your thumb and forefinger. The length you want to extend beyond the bend of the hook (1 shank length) should be hidden inside your fingers. Hold the fibers at a 45° angle to the shank of the hook, just above where the thread is hanging, with the trimmed butt ends pointing toward you. Start winding the thread over the fibers, rotating them parallel to the shank of the hook for the first few winds. Keep winding evenly toward the eye until you're at the middle of the shank. Wind back evenly to the bend.

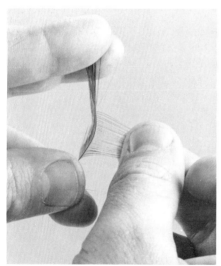

Step 1.

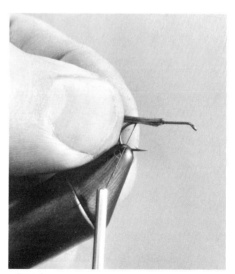

Step 2.

Step 3: Use a premixed olive dubbing or make your own from a piece of olive-dyed rabbit or Zonker strip. Cut the fur from the hide, pull out the long guard hairs and mix, tease, and remix the fur to get it all fluffed up. Dub a very thin fur body with just a slight amount of taper. For most dry flies, separate the fur into small loose puffs and barely ''dirty'' the thread with the dubbing. Use lots of pressure when you dub. Wind the dubbed body forward for 2/3 of the hook shank. Remove or add a little dubbing as needed.

Step 4: Select two blue dun dry fly hackles. To select feathers without removing them from the cape, hold the cape in front of the hook with the feathered side facing the hook and carefully fan a feather around the bottom of the hook. It should flare to about 1½ to 2

hook gapes long. When you find the right size, pull that feather and one next to it from the cape. Strip the fibers from the bottom ends of both feathers — usually come up to a point where the center web is less than 1/3 of the total width of the hackle. Strip off the lower fibers just as you plucked the tail fibers.

Step 5: Tie in both feathers on top of the hook shank, dull sides facing up, and tips pointing toward the tails. Leave a small amount of stem between the feather and the tie-in point. Wind forward over the stems smoothly, stopping about 1/16'' from the eye of the hook and trim the remaining stems. The thread should be left hanging just behind the eye of the hook.

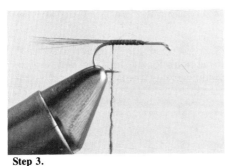

Step 3.

Step 4.

Step 5.

Step 6: Grasp the tip of the top hackle with a pair of hackle pliers and wind it away from you, dull side forward, in tight turns with just a tiny space between each turn. The first turn should fall tight against the body. If the hackle doesn't want to wind dull side forward, back it up a bit, twist the hackle pliers, and try again. If the hackle slips out of the pliers or breaks, just grasp it further down and start over (don't let this frustrate you, some hackles just break more easily than others). Tie off the hackle just behind the eye of the hook on top of the shank.

Step 7: Wind the second hackle carefully through the gaps you left when winding the first hackle. Tie it off in the same place, whip finish, and apply a drop of head cement to the head.

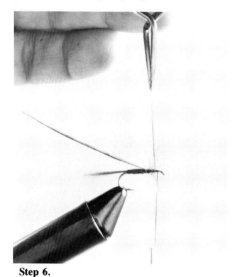

Step 6.

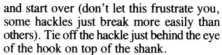

Step 7.

Light Cahill Dry Fly

The Light Cahill is a classic Catskill dry fly, one of the most popular dries to use when cream-colored mayflies are hatching. It is slightly more complicated than the Blue-Wing Olive, in that it features upright wings of wood duck flank feathers. Handling these feathers is one of the toughest accomplishments in dry fly tying, but a lot of patterns call for this kind of wing. A lot of problems with wood duck wings stem from material preparation and selection, so pay close attention to steps 2 and 3, to a size 12 dry fly hook.

Step 1: Select and tie in a bunch of cream or light ginger hackle fibers to a size 12 dry fly hook for tails, exactly as you did for the

Blue-Wing Olive. Advance the thread to a point about 1/4 of a hook shank length behind the eye.

Step 2: Select a wood duck flank feather, or mallard feather dyed to match wood duck, in which there are nicely formed, even tips distributed equally around both sides of the stem. At each side of the feather, you'll see where the nice even ends grade into soft, webby fibers. Strip the webby fibers away. Come down about 3/4 to 1/2'' from the top of the feather, and with the very tip of your scissors, snip out the center stem. Now work the feather around in your hand, folding the two sides together, until all the ends line up. Come down about 1'' from the tips and snip the rest of the feather off.

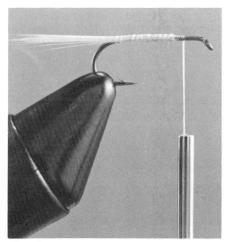

Step 1.

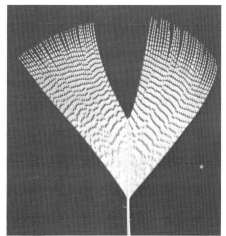

Step 2.

Step 3: Measure the clump of wood duck feathers against the hook shank — one shank length, including the fine untrimmed ends should extend beyond your thumb and forefinger. Hold the feathers just above the top of the hook shank, extending over the eye of the fly, and tie them in with the pinch method. Repeat for 3 or 4 pinches. Trim the butt ends, beyond the windings, on an angle and wind the thread back over the butt ends and then back in front of the wing.

Step 4: Pull the wing fibers straight upright and wind some tight turns of thread directly in front of them. 8 or 10 turns should do it — let go of the wing and see if it stays in place. If not, raise it up and take a few more turns.

Step 5: Using a dubbing needle or the point of your scissors, split the fibers into two equal bunches. Pull each bunch off to one side. Wind the thread in a figure-8 motion between them by crossing over the top of the hook to the back of the far wing, underneath the hook, and back between the wings on top of the hook. The fibers should be equally split into two wings.

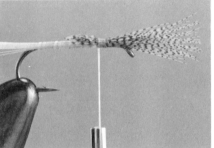

Step 3.

Step 4.

Step 5.

Step 6: Wind once around the base of each wing to keep the fibers in place: holding the far wing, wind around the hook in front of the wing, carefully once around the base of the far wing in a clockwise direction, underneath the hook (keep very light pressure on the thread), then grab the near wing and go clockwise around the base of it (this is the tricky part, keep very light pressure on the thread), then take a complete turn around the shank in front of the wing. Now let go of the near wing. You should be left with two neatly cocked wings.

Step 7: Run the thread back to the bend of the hook and dub a thin fur body of cream fox fur (follow directions for the Blue-Wing Olive previously). Stop the body a little more than 1/16'' behind the wings.

Step 8: Tie in two cream or light ginger dry fly hackles behind the wing. Prepare and tie them in exactly as for the Blue-Wing Olive. Trim the butt ends of the hackles just behind the wing and wind them forward, with about equal turns behind and in front of the wing. Don't wind the hackles between the wings, just make a turn behind the wings and then in front as you pass by them. The first hackle should be tied mostly behind the wing, with 2 or 3 turns in front; then the second hackle should be spiraled quickly through the hackle behind the wings and concentrated in front of them. Tie off the hackles, whip finish, and apply head cement as for the Blue-Wing Olive.

Step 6.

Step 7.

Step 8.

Eleven Basic Flies that Will Teach You to Tie   21

The Blue Dun Wet

The Blue Dun Wet fly has been around for almost 300 years, the pattern basically unchanged. It imitates many drowned or emerging insects, and is a favorite fly to use when nothing appears to be going on. It is best in sizes 10 through 16.

Techniques Learned: Wet fly hackle
Wet fly wing
Beard hackle

Step 1: Start your thread — gray or white — in the middle of a size 10 standard wet fly hook. Tie in blue dun hackle fiber tails and dub a body of gray fur (muskrat, gray fox, rabbit), using the same techniques you did for the Blue-Wing Olive dry. The difference with a wet fly is that the tails should be shorter (about 1/2 of the shank length), sparser, and can be tied with webby fibers. The body should be a little more heavily tapered, fatter at the front end. Stop the body about 1/4'' from the eye for a size 10 hook.

Step 2: Select a webby blue dun hackle whose fibers are about the length of the hook gape. You can use the same sizing method as you did for the Blue-Wing Olive dry. For a wet fly, we like to use a feather that is at least half web. You can use hen hackles, poor quality dry fly hackle, or the bottom half of a better quality dry fly hackle. Holding the tip of the hackle, stroke the fibers down toward the butt until they are about 90° from the stem. Tie the tip of the hackle to the top of the hook, shiny side up, just in front of the body with a half dozen tight turns of thread. Trim any excess tip.

Step 3: Grasp the butt end of the hackle with your hackle pliers and hold it straight above the hook. Moisten your fingers slightly and stroke the hackle fibers back until they are all on one side of the stem (toward the rear of the fly). Now wind the hackle, advancing slightly forward on each turn, stroking the hackle fibers back as you go, and constantly adjusting with the hackle pliers so the fibers slant to the rear. Don't wind all the way to the eye, stop about 1/16'' back from the eye. Tie off the hackle underneath the shank of the hook with four tight turns and trim the excess hackle tip.

Step 1.

Step 2.

Step 3.

Step 4: Place your thumb and forefinger on top of the hackle and pull them down and back while pinching the hackle. This will pull most of the fibers under the hook, pointing to the rear. Holding the hackle in place, wind the thread back over the hackle just a little — about 1/32'' — so that most of the hackle stays underneath the hook. Three or four turns will usually do it.

Step 5: An optional method for winding wet fly hackle is to use a beard hackle. Pluck a bunch of webby hackle from a large hen hackle, hen saddle, or from the bottom of a webby saddle hackle. Turn the fly over in the vise and tie in the bunch with the pinch method. The fibers should extend about 3/4 of the way to the point of the hook. Trim the scrap ends.

Step 6: Select a matched pair of gray duck quills — mallard, teal, pintail, wood duck, and black duck all work fine. Make sure they are a matched pair — their curvatures will be mirror images of each other. Snip a section from each feather, just slightly narrower than the gape of the hook (about 3/16'' wide for a size 10 hook.) The wings on a size 10 hook will be about 7/16'' long — about as long as the shank of the hook — and this entire portion must be free of the shiny blood line that extends from the center of the quill. If you wind thread over the blood line the wing will "accordian" and won't tie in properly. Carefully place the matched wings together, concave sides facing each other. It may help to wet your fingers when you handle the wings.

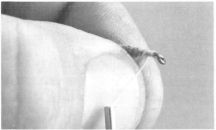

Step 4.

Step 5.

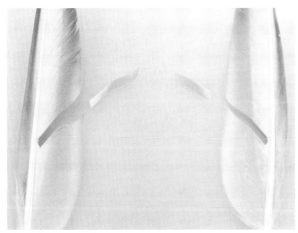

Step 6.

Step 7: Notice that, as you hold the wings horizontally, they have a long side and a short side. Place the matched wings over the top of the hook, long sides up, with the end of the wing extending just to the bend of the hook. Bring them down onto the hook until they just barely straddle the hook. Holding them in place with your thumb and forefinger, bring a loose loop of thread up and over them. The easiest way to do this is to pinch them in place, rock your fingers back onto the first knuckle to open them up, form

a loop of thread, and rock them back over the thread. Pinch the wings, thread, and hook together and pull down with the thread to tighten the loop. Repeat the process three or four times.

Step 8: Trim the butt ends of the wing carefully while still holding the wing in place and wind over the butt ends. Don't wind back over the wing as you'll ruin the set of the wings if you do so. Form a neat head, whip finish, and apply a drop of head cement.

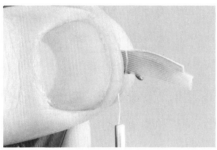

Step 7.

Step 8.

The Black Nose Dace Bucktail

This is a traditional bucktail, an imitation of one of the most common trout stream minnows. Big trout eat a lot of them. It is usually tied fairly small and sparse, sizes 6 through 12, and is an effective fly even in low clear water.

Techniques Learned: Tinsel body
Oval tinsel rib
Bucktail wing

Step 1: Clamp a size 6 streamer hook in your vise and start black thread about 1/3 of the way back from the eye of the hook. Wind the thread back to the bend of the hook. Cut a 2'' piece of thin red wool or acrylic yarn and a 5'' piece of oval silver tinsel. Tie in the red wool with 2 turns of thread, letting about 1/2'' extend beyond the bend and the rest extending all the way past the eye of the hook. Tie in the oval tinsel with another two turns in the same place, with 1½ inches of the tinsel extending over the eye of the hook and the rest sticking out beyond the bend. Trim both the tinsel and the wool together on an angle, about 3/16'' back from the eye of the hook. Wind the thread forward in smooth turns, covering the tinsel and wool and smoothing over any bumps with extra turns of thread.

Step 2: Pull a 7'' piece of medium silver tinsel from the spool and cut it on an angle at one end. Tie the tinsel in just ahead of the place where the wool and oval tinsel end, covering half of the slanted angle of tinsel that you have just trimmed. This will help you start winding the tinsel without forming a bump.

Step 3: Wind the tinsel to the bend of the hook, covering all the thread windings. Each turn should butt against the previous one, but not overlap. Then wind the tinsel back over itself in the same manner, back to the tie-in point. Tie off the flat tinsel with 5 or 6 firm wraps on the underside of the hook.

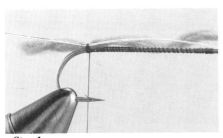

Step 1.

Step 2.

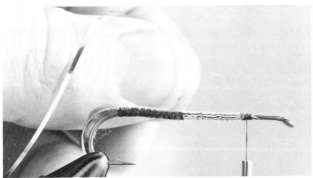

Step 3.

Step 4: Snip the wool tail to about 1/4" long. Wind the oval tinsel forward in even spirals over the flat tinsel. Tie off on the underside of the hook.

Step 5: From a natural brown and white bucktail, snip a bunch of white hairs from near the tip of the bucktail, about 1/4" in diameter. Holding the hair by the tips, pull away from the tips with the thumb and forefinger of your other hand to remove any fuzz and short hairs from the butt ends of the bucktail. Place the bucktail, tip ends down, into a hair stacker and rap the stacker sharply on a hard surface a dozen times or so to even up the ends. Hold the stacker horizontally, remove the brass tube slowly, and pull the evened bucktail out by the tip ends. (Note:

this can also be done by hand, by pulling short fibers out of the clamp and placing them back, even with the longer tips — in fact if your bucktail is not thoroughly cleaned it may be a necessity.)

Step 6: Bring your thread to a point midway between where the tinsel body stops and the eye of the hook. Hold the white bucktail on top of the hook and adjust it until the tip ends extend to about 1/2 shank length (1-1/8") beyond the bend. Tie the hair in with the pinch method. Repeat 3 or 4 times. Snip the butt ends of the hair on an angle, extending almost to the eye. Wind toward the eye over the butts, back to the tinsel body, and then forward to just behind where you tied the first bunch in.

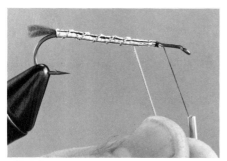

Step 4.

Step 5.

Step 6.

Step 7: Prepare a bunch of dyed black bucktail in the same manner, tie in, cut the butts on an angle parallel to the first butts, wind to the eye, back to the tinsel and back to a point just behind where the second bunch was tied in.

Step 8: Tie a bunch of natural brown bucktail in, using the same technique. Wind a smooth neat head, whip finish, and apply several drops of head cement, letting the cement work back slightly into the hair to keep it from slipping out.

Step 7.

Step 8.

Eleven Basic Flies that Will Teach You to Tie   27

The Irresistible Dry Fly

The Irresistible is a great fly for fast, bubbly water. Its bulky silhouette will catch a trout's attention in fast water, and the hollow deer hair body means that if the fly is drowned, it will pop back up. This version is the Adams Irresistible — Adams wings and hackle with a hair body and tail.

Techniques Learned: Hair tail
                        Deer hair body
                        Hackle tip wings

Step 1: Attach black, white, or tan 3/0 monocord to a size 10 dry fly hook, just ahead of the bend. Using the pinch method, but with less pressure than usual for the first couple turns, tie in a bunch of brown bucktail, dark elk, or elk hock — any stiff hair that won't flare. The tail should be slightly shorter than normal; about 3/4 shank length. Instead of binding the tails to the hook for half the shank length, cut the butt ends off as short as you can while still holding the hair so it won't pull out. Flaring

deer hair, which we'll do in the next couple of steps, is easier to do on a bare hook.

Step 2: For the size 10 hook you're using, snip a bunch of deer body hair from the hide, about the diameter of a pencil. Holding the tips of the hairs with the thumb and forefinger of one hand, pull the short hairs and fuzz out of the butt ends of the hair with the thumb and forefinger of the other hand. Snip the fine tips of the hair off, so you're left with a bunch of deer hair with both ends squared off, about 3/4'' long, a little less than the diameter of a pencil.

Step 3: Hold the hair at a 45° angle to the shank of the hook as shown. Take a loose loop around the middle of the hair, applying just a tiny amount of pressure. Hold onto the hair. Take a second turn in the same spot, a little tighter, and begin to release the hair. Take a third turn with as much pressure as you can without breaking the thread and let go of the hair. It will flare around the hook. If it doesn't cover the entire 360°, spread it around a little with your fingers.

Step 1.

Step 2.

Step 3.

Step 4: Come around in front of the hair with the thread, push the hair back toward the bend a little with your fingernails, and wind 6 or 8 tight turns just in front of it. Repeat the hair flaring with a second, slightly larger bunch of hair. The second bunch will flare easier because its over bare hook. You should now have the rear half of the hook covered with deer hair — if not add a small bunch. Push the hair back a little, wind in front of it, whip finish, and remove the hook from the vise.

Step 5: With a pair of sharp scissors (those with serrated blades work far better than normal scissors), trim the deer hair body. Cut from the front of the fly to the back, angling the scissors to get a slight taper. Be careful not to cut the tails! The body should be about 1/8 - 3/16'' in diameter for our size 10 hook. Deer hair can also be trimmed with a very sharp razor blade, but we've never found it to be as effective as serrated blade scissors. After you're done trimming the body, reattach your thread just in front of the body.

Step 6: Select two grizzly hackles about 1/16'' to 1/8'' wide, with nicely rounded tips. Measure down one shank length, about 1/2'', from the tips and trim away the fibers from the stem, leaving a small stubble . . . this will keep the wings from pulling out when you bind them in.

Step 4.

Step 5.

Step 6.

Step 7: Tie in the hackle tips with the pinch method, halfway between the eye of the hook and the forward end of the body, facing over the eye. Raise them upright and wind 4 or 5 times in front to hold them up — it will take less thread than the wood duck wings on the Light Cahill. Wind a figure-8 between the wings as you did with the Light Cahill — but you don't need to take a turn around the bases. Wind back to the deer hair, binding the stubbly hackle butts under, and trim away any excess hackle butt.

Step 8: Tie in two brown and one grizzly hackle with fibers that are 1 ½ - 2 hook gapes in length, binding the stems under to just behind the wing. Bring the thread forward to just behind the eye, wind the hackles, whip finish, and apply a drop of head cement to the head. (Note: if you have a long brown hackle or a saddle hackle that is 1 ½ - 2 hook gapes in length when wound, use just one brown hackle. With normal neck hackle, though, you really need 3 hackle to tie a nice bushy Irresistible.

Step 7.

Step 8.

The Parachute Hare's Ear Dry

The Parachute Hare's Ear is a buggy look-ing dry fly that is very attractive to trout. The upright white wing makes it highly visible in fast water or in the evening, and the parachute hackle ensures that it will float upright every time. Parachutes float low in the water, presenting a larger profile to the trout, and are often more effective than high-floating dry flies.

Techniques Learned: Hair wing
Parachute hackle

Step 1: Start your black or white thread in the center of a size 12 dry fly hook. Wind back to the bend. Snip a bunch of dark elk or elk hock hairs, clean the fuzz and small hairs from the butt ends and even the ends in a stacker if you wish. Tie them in with the pinch method, using light pressure for the first few turns to keep them from flaring too much. The tails should extend about 3/4 of a shank length beyond the bend. Snip the butt ends at about the midpoint of the shank and wind forward smoothly to cover them.

Step 2: Snip a large bunch of calf body hair, about 1/4'' in diameter, and clean all the fuzz and short hairs from the butts by holding tightly to the tips and stroking the butts with your other hand. (The hair will shrink down to about 3/16'' after you clean it.) Place the hair in a stacker, tips down, and rap sharply a dozen times on a hard surface. Holding the stacker horizontally, remove the brass tube and grasp the tips of the hair.

Step 3: Advance your thread to a point about 1/3 shank length behind the eye. Wind back and forth a couple of times just behind the eye so the hair wing won't slip after you tie it in. Tie in the stack of calf body hair, about 1 shank length long, extending over the eye of the hook. Use about 8 tight turns. Raise the hair upright and wind about a dozen turns of thread tightly in front of the wing. Trim the butts so they meet where the tail winds left off for a neat underbody, and wind the thread back over the butts and then return to just behind the wing.

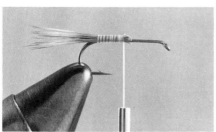

Step 1.

Step 2.

Step 3.

Step 4: Wind the thread around the very bottom of the wing about 5 or 6 times to gather the hairs into a neat bunch. (Note: if you were tying a Wulff or other hair wing fly, at this point you could divide the wing with a figure-8 wind as you did with the Light Cahill and wind around the base of each wing to create two nicely cocked wings. The parachute, however, uses a single upright wing.)

Step 5: Wind back to the bend, dub a tapered body of hare's ear fur, and wind the body forward to just in front of the wing.

Step 6: Tie in a single grizzly hackle, shiny side up, with fibers that are 1½ - 2 times the length of the gape of the hook just in front of the wing.

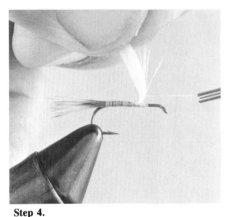

Step 4.

Step 6.

Step 5.

Step 7: Grasp the hackle with a pair of hackle pliers and wind it counter-clockwise (as you look down on the wing) around the base of the wing. The best way to do this is to jump the hackle up to about 1/16'' up onto the wing, and then wind down toward the body with successive winds. When you reach the body, bring the hackle around the front of the wing, pass the hackle pliers over the shank and let them hang there. Then, stroke all the hackles back out of the way with one hand and tie in the hackle just in front of the wing with your other hand.

Step 8: Dub about a 3/4'' length of your thread with hare's ear fur. Pull the hackle back out of the way again and cover the forward portion of the shank of the hook with the fur. Wind a small head, whip finish (whip finish at a more horizontal angle than normal to keep from winding the parachute hackle under), and apply a drop of head cement to the head.

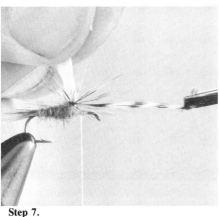

Step 7.

Step 8.

The Muddler Minnow

The Muddler Minnow is, like the Woolly Bugger, famous for the many large trout it has fooled. It can be fished dry, well greased, as a hopper or stonefly imitation. But it is most useful fished weighted or on a sinking tip line, as an imitation of the sculpin, a small fish that is a favorite prey of large trout. The Muddler is deadly in size 2 all the way down to tiny size 12's.

Techniques Learned: Feather tail
Feather wing with hair underwing
Deer hair head and collar

Step 1: Start with 3/0 monocord about 1/3 of the shank length back from the eye. Wind back to the bend of the hook. From a matched pair of mottled turkey wing quill secondary, snip a piece from the right and the left wing quill, about 3/16'' wide. Match the quills, concave sides together, and tie in using the pinch method. The tails should ex-

tend about 1/2'' beyond the bend of the hook. Snip the butt ends of the feathers at the point where you started your thread, wind the thread forward evenly over the ends of the quills trying to keep them from rolling under the hook — this will make your tinsel body neater.

Step 2: At the point where your thread was started, tie in a 8-10'' long piece of medium gold tinsel and wind to the bend and back, just as you did for the Black Nose Dace. Tie off the tinsel under the shank of the hook.

Step 3: From a gray squirrel tail, pull a bunch of hairs about 3/16'' in diameter perpendicular to the center bone of the tail until the tips of the hair are relatively even. Hold them here and snip them off the tail. Clean the butt ends of fuzz and short hairs, cut the butt ends off so you have a bunch of hair about 2½'' long, and tie in right where the tinsel body ends with the pinch method. Trim the butt ends close to the tie-in point and bind them under with thread.

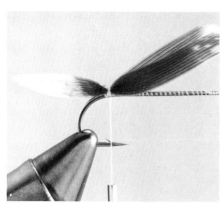

Step 1.

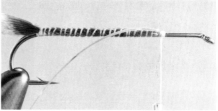

Step 2.

Step 3.

Step 4: Cut two more pieces of mottled turkey quill, about 5/16'' wide, one from each side of a matched pair. Place one feather on the far side of the hook, against the squirrel tail, so the tip extends almost to the end of the tail. The quill should just barely straddle the hook at the tie-in point. The concave side should be facing you. Hold it in place with your index finger and place the other feather on the near side of the hook, concave side facing the other feather. The feathers should envelope the squirrel hair. Tie in both feathers with the pinch method. Use about a half dozen pinches to hold them in place, then trim the butts to 1/4'' and bind them under with thread.

Step 5: Cut a bunch of deer body hair, a little less than a pencil in diameter. Clean the fuzz and loose hairs from the butt ends and place in a stacker to even the ends. Trim the butt ends so the hair measures about 3/4'' long. Turn the hook upside down in the vise, hold the hair so that about 1/2'' of the tips extend beyond the wing tie-in point, and tie in using a fairly loose pinch, holding your fingers on the sides of the hook. The hair should flare around the bottom of the hook, forming a collar. Push the butt ends back toward the wing and wind 6 or 8 very tight turns up against the hair to push it back.

Step 6: Turn the hook back over in the vise and form a collar on top of the hook in the exact same manner.

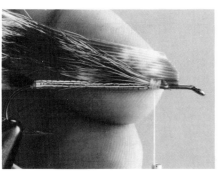

Step 4.

Step 5.

Step 6.

Step 7: With a similar-sized bunch of deer hair, cut both the tips and the butts so you're left with some deer hair that has both ends squared off. Tie it in just ahead of the collar, letting this bunch flare completely around the hook, as you did for the Irresistible body. Push the hair back with your fingernails, wind a dozen tight turns in front of it, form a neat head, and whip finish.

Step 8: Remove the hook from the vise and trim the head with a pair of serrated-blade scissors forming a bullet shape tapering from the collar to the eye. Don't cut the fine collar away — if you've followed our instructions for spinning the hair it should be easy to distinguish between the finely tapered collar, which should not be trimmed, and the blunt ends of the head, which should be trimmed.

Step 7.

Step 8.

The Crazy Charlie Bonefish Fly

The Crazy Charlie is one of the deadliest new bonefish flies to be developed in years. It is especially effective on Christmas Island in the Pacific in tan, brown, and pink, but will catch bonefish wherever they are found. The bead chain eyes help to sink the fly quickly to an effective level. Tied on top of the hook shank, the eyes make the fly ride upside-down, keeping it from snagging on the bottom.

Techniques Learned: Tinsel body over-wrapped with Body Glass
Bead Chain eyes
Calf tail wing

Step 1: Attach white 3/0 thread to the front 1/3 of a Mustad 34007 stainless hook, size 4, 6, or 8. Leave the thread hanging at a point about 1/3 shank length back from the eye. With a pair of wire cutters, snip 2 brass or nickel-plated beads from a length of bead chain. Hold them in place above the hook and make about 8 figure-8 turns around the center shaft that holds the beads together. Then wind about 6 turns of thread horizontally around the base of the eyes to help lock the thread and hold them in place. These turns should be made as tight as possible.

Step 2: Bring the thread behind the eyes. Cut a 5" piece of clear Body Glass. Bind it to the shank of the hook. Note that the Body Glass has a flat side and a round side. Tie it in so that the flat side is facing up and the round side down. Bind it under with smooth even turns to the bend of the hook, then return the thread to behind the eyes. Leave the Body Glass hanging off the back of the fly.

Step 3: Tie in an 8" piece of wide pearlescent tinsel just behind the eye. Wind the tinsel in smooth, non-overlapping turns that just touch the preceding turn, back to the bend and then back to behind the eyes. Tie off four or five tight turns of thread.

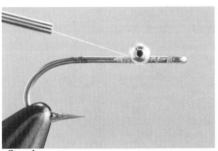

Step 1.

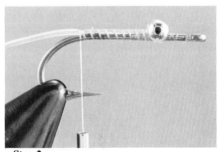

Step 2.

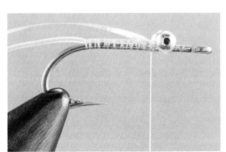

Step 3.

Step 4: Bring the thread around in front of the eyes. Wind the Body Glass, round side up in turns that just touch the preceding one forward. When you get to the eyes, bring the Body Glass between the eyes and tie off on top of the hook shank with 6 to 8 very tight turns of thread. Trim the excess Body Glass.

Step 5: Search through a tan calf tail for a spot where the tips are relatively even with each other. Grasp a bunch that is about 1/4''

in diameter and pull the bunch away from the center bone of the tail until the tips appear to be evenly aligned. Snip the hairs from the tail.

Step 6: Holding the tips of the hair clean the fuzz and short hairs from the base. Then hold the hair by the butts and remove any hairs that are longer than the main part of the bunch. You should be left with a bunch of hairs about 1/8'' in diameter.

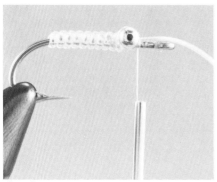

Step 4.

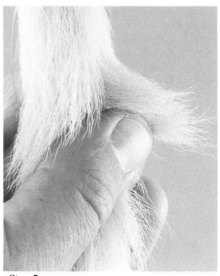

Step 5.

Step 6.

Step 7: Turn the hook over in the vise. With the pinch method, tie the hair onto the hook, with the tips extending just barely beyond the bend of the hook. Snip the butts of the hair on a relatively sharp angle and wind tightly over the butt ends of the hair.

Step 8: Wind a neatly tapered head, whip finish, and apply head cement. When you cement the head, apply a couple of drops to the underside of the bead eyes (where the Body Glass crossed over), and also let the cement work into the base of the wing slightly.

Step 7.

Step 8.

The Deceiver Saltwater Streamer

The Deceiver, developed by the incomparable Lefty Kreh, is the most useful, most versatile saltwater fly ever developed. Tied in sizes 8 through 4/0, it will catch almost any saltwater fish that will take a fly. It can be tied in almost any combination of colors, but the most popular is white, with a peacock herl topping as we've shown here.

Techniques Learned: Large hackle tail/ wing
Bucktail collar
Tinsel sides
Peacock herl topping

Step 1: You'll need some large white hackles for this fly. The very best are the wide hackles at the top of a wet fly or streamer neck. Second best are wide saddle hackles. Just make sure that the hackles you choose have a heavy, stiff stem. If you use regular skinny saddles with thin stems, the feathers will wrap around the bend of the hook making the fly spin when you retrieve

it. Select 4 or 6 or 8 feathers with a similar shape (you'll need even numbers because they will be placed concave sides together to get a balanced fly). The size you need depends on how long you want your fly to be, but 2'' to 6'' is a common range. Strip the fuzz from the bases of the hackles and split them into two groups, then (assuming the wing will have four feathers) put two of them with the concave side facing the convex side of the other, and repeat for the other two. Then place the concave sides of the two groups facing each other — leaving you with a flat bunch of four feathers. Attach black 3/0 monocord to the middle of the hook and wind back to the bend. Make sure you go back all the way to the point where the bend starts to curve over, otherwise, again, the wing will wrap around the hook. Arrange the feathers so that the stems are parallel and tie them in, all in one bunch, using the pinch method. Wind forward smoothly over the stems to a point 1/3 shank length back from the eye.

Step 1.

Step 2: Tie in a piece of medium or wide silver tinsel. Wind back to the bend and then return to the tie-in point.

Step 3: Turn the hook over in the vise. Select a large bunch of white bucktail, clean the ends, and even them up as you did with the Black Nose Dace. Tie the bunch in right where the tinsel body stopped with 3 or 4 pinches, then trim the butt ends of the hair just behind the eye and wind tightly over the butts. This hair should almost encircle the bottom 180° of the hook shank.

Step 2.

Step 3.

Step 4: Turn the hook back over and tie in a second bunch of hair exactly as you did the first. Important: The hair should extend *beyond* the bend of the hook as shown, as it will help to keep the wing from wrapping around the bend. Cut two pieces of silver tinsel that are as long as the fly. Hold one against the fly on the near side, just behind the head, and wind thread over four or five times. Turn the fly over in the vise (or just reach over the top) and tie in the second piece of tinsel on the other side.

Step 5: Tie in 3 or 4 peacock herls from just below the eyed portion of a peacock tail (the herls are widest here) on top of the bucktail. Instead of using the pinch method, it's easiest to just hold them in place and carefully wind the thread over them. Wind forward to the eye of the hook, then gradually work back toward the bucktail, tapering the head as you go. Whip finish in the center of the head. Apply two coats of head cement to the head.

Step 4.

Step 5.

PART II

Index
of Orvis
Fly Patterns

CHAPTER I DRY AND WET FLIES

ORVIS DRY FLIES ... Opening Comments

Dubbed Bodies
Synthetic materials may be substituted for natural furs provided that the colors are compatible.I will leave the choice up to you, since the whole subject is very controversial.

Quill Bodies
Stripped Grizzly Hackle Quills may be substituted where Stripped Peacock is required. Stripped Grizzly Hackle Quills are much more durable and produce a finely segmented body.

Quill Fiber Bodies
This body style is required for the Borcher Special and the Fluttering Caddis. It is accomplished by wrapping 2 to 4 fibers, stripped from a wing or tail quill. See Fluttering Caddis tying instructions on page 169

Hackle Comments
Dry Fly Hackle should be used . . . either Grade A or B. Only natural or photo dyed duns and natural or cold dyed blacks are recommended.

Polywing Spinners
The wings should be tied very sparsely to maintain translucency.

Wood Duck Wings
Natural Wood Duck and Orvis Mallard dyed Wood Duck are recommended.

Adams

Hook	Orvis Premium or equivalent.
Size	10 to 20
Thread	Gray - 6/0 Pre-Waxed
Wings	Grizzly Hackle Tips - Upright and Divided.
Tail	Brown and Grizzly Hackle Fibers mixed.
Body	Muskrat or Medium Gray Poly.
Hackle	Brown and Grizzly mixed.

Borcher Special

Hook	Orvis Premium or equivalent.
Size	12 to 18
Thread	Gray - 6/0 Pre-Waxed.
Wings	Lt. Dun Hackle Tips - Upright and Divided.
Tail	Mahogany Ringneck Pheasant Tail Fibers.
Rib	Gold Wire
Body	Oak Turkey Wing Quill Fibers.
Hackle	Brown and Grizzly mixed.

Mosquito

Hook	Orvis Premium or equivalent.
Size	12 to 20
Thread	Gray - 6/0 Pre-Waxed.
Wing	Grizzly Hackle Tips - Upright and Divided.
Tail	Grizzly Hackle Fibers.
Body	Stripped Grizzly Hackle Quill.
Hackle	Grizzly.

Pale Evening Dun

Hook	Orvis Premium or equivalent.
Size	14 to 20
Thread	Cream - 6/0 Pre-Waxed.
Wings	Lt. Dun Hackle Tips - Upright and Divided.
Tail	Lt. Dun Hackle Fibers.
Body	Pale Yellow Dubbing or Poly.
Hackle	Lt. Dun.

Blue Wing Olive

Hook	Orvis Premium or equivalent.
Size	14 to 20
Thread	Olive - 6/0 Pre-Waxed.
Wing	Dark Dun Hackle Tips - Upright and Divided.
Tail	Dark Dun Hackle Fibers.
Body	Medium Olive Fur or Poly.
Hackle	Dark Dun

Blue Quill

Hook	Orvis Premuim or equivalent.
Size	12 to 18
Thread	Gray - 6/0 Pre-Waxed.
Wing	Mallard Wing Quill Segments or Med. Dun Hackle Tips - Upright and Divided.
Tail	Medium Dun Hackle Fibers.
Rib	Fine Gold Wire.
Body	Stripped Peacock Quill.
Hackle	Medium Dun.

Dark Hendrickson

Hook	Orvis Premium or equivalent.
Size	12 to 18
Thread	Gray - 6/0 Pre-Waxed.
Wing	Lemon Wood Duck - Upright and Divided.
Tail	Dark Dun Hackle Fibers.
Body	Dark Muskrat or Med. Gray Poly
Hackle	Dark Dun

Light Hendrickson

Hook	Orvis Premium or equivalent.
Size	12 to 18
Thread	Tan - 6/0 Pre-Waxed.
Wing	Lemon Wood Duck - Upright and Divided.
Tail	Med. Dun Hackle Fibers.
Body	Pinkish Fox Fur or Poly.
Hackle	Medium Dun.

Brown May Fly

Hook	Orvis Premium or equivalent
Size	12 to 16
Thread	Tan - 6/0 Pre-Waxed.
Wing	Lemon Wood Duck - Upright and Divided.
Tail	Mahogany Ringneck Pheasant Tail Fibers.
Rib	Stripped Peacock Quill.
Body	Tan Raffia or equivalent.
Hackle	Brown.

Quill Gordon

Hook	Orvis Premium or equivalent.
Size	12 to 18
Thread	Cream - 6/0 Pre-Waxed.
Wing	Lemon Wood Duck - Upright and Divided.
Tail	Med. Dun Hackle Fibers.
Rib	Fine Gold Wire.
Body	Stripped Peacock Quill.
Hackle	Medium Dun.

Dark Cahill

Hook	Orvis Premium or equivalent.
Size	12 to 18.
Thread	Tan - 6/0 Pre-Waxed.
Wing	Lemon Wood Duck - Upright and Divided.
Tail	Brown Hackle Fibers.
Body	Muskrat Fur or Med. Gray Poly.
Hackle	Brown.

Fan-Wing Royal Coachman

Hook	Orvis Premium or equivalent.
Size	8 to 12.
Thread	Black - 6/0 Pre-Waxed.
Wing	Fan Shaped Wood Duck Breast - Upright and Divided.
Tail	Golden Pheasant Tippet or Coachman Brown Hackle Fibers.
Body	Peacock Herl with Red Floss Center Band.
Hackle	Coachman Brown.

Red Quill

Hook   Orvis Premium or equivalent.
Size   12 to 18
Thread   Olive - 6/0 Pre-Waxed.
Wing   Lemon Wood Duck - Upright and Divided.
Tail   Med. Dun Hackle Fibers.
Body   Stripped Coachman Brown Hackle Quill.
Hackle   Medium Dun.

Light Cahill

Hook   Orvis Premium or equivalent.
Size   12 to 20
Thread   Yellow - 6/0 Pre-Waxed.
Wing   Lemon Wood Duck - Upright and Divided.
Tail   Dark Cream Hackle Fibers.
Body   Cream Fur or Poly.
Hackle   Dark Cream.

Gray Fox

Hook   Orvis Premium or equivalent.
Size   12 to 18
Thread   Yellow - 6/0 Pre-Waxed.
Wing   Gray Mallard Flank - Upright and Divided.
Tail   Golden Ginger Hackle Fibers.
Body   Tan Fur or Poly.
Hackle   Golden Ginger and Grizzly mixed.

March Brown

Hook   Orvis Premium or equivalent.
Size   12 to 16
Thread   Yellow - 6/0 Pre-Waxed.
Wing   Lemon Wood Duck - Upright and Divided.
Tail   Brown Hackle Fibers.
Body   Fawn Fox Fur or Poly.
Hackle   Brown and Grizzly mixed.

Cream Variant

Hook	Orvis Premium or equivalent.
Size	10 to 22
Thread	Yellow - 6/0 Pre-Waxed.
Tail	Dark Cream Hackle Fibers.
Body	Stripped Dark Cream Hackle Quill.
Hackle	Dark Cream Saddle Hackle.

Gray Fox Variant

Hook	Orvis Premium or equivalent.
Size	10 to 22
Thread	Yellow - 6/0 Pre-Waxed.
Tail	Golden Ginger Hackle Fibers.
Body	Stripped Dark Cream Hackle Quill.
Hackle	Golden Ginger, Dark Ginger and Grizzly Saddle Hackle mixed.

Dun Variant

Hook	Orvis Premium or equivalent.
Size	10 to 22
Thread	Olive - 6/0 Pre-Waxed.
Tail	Dark Dun Hackle Fibers.
Body	Stripped Coachman Brown Hackle Quill.
Hackle	Dark Dun Saddle Hackle.

Brown Bivisible

Hook	Orvis Premium or equivalent.
Size	10 to 14.
Thread	Black - 6/0 Pre-Waxed.
Tail	Brown Hackle Fibers.
Body	Three Brown Hackles increasing in size tightly palmered from tail to head.
Hackle	Cream - three turns.

Ginger Quill

Hook	Orvis Premium or equivalent.
Size	12 to 18
Thread	Cream - 6/0 Pre-Waxed.
Wing	Mallard Wing Quill Segments - Upright and Divided.
Tail	Dark Cream Hackle Fibers.
Rib	Fine Gold Wire.
Body	Stripped Peacock Quill.
Hackle	Dark Cream.

Black Gnat

Hook	Orvis Premium or equivalent.
Size	12 to 18
Thread	Black - 6/0 Pre-Waxed.
Wing	Mallard Wing Quill Segments - Upright and Divided.
Tail	Black Hackle Fibers.
Body	Black Fur or Poly.
Hackle	Black.

Royal Coachman

Hook	Orvis Premium or equivalent.
Size	10 to 18
Thread	Black - 6/0 Pre-Waxed.
Wing	White Duck Wing Quill Segments - Upright and Divided.
Tail	Golden Pheasant Tippet or Coachman Brown Hackle Fibers.
Body	Peacock Herl with a Red Floss Center Band.
Hackle	Coachman Brown.

Blue Dun

Hook	Orvis Premium or equivalent.
Size	12 to 18
Thread	Gray - 6/0 Pre-Waxed.
Wing	Mallard Wing Quill Segments - Upright and Divided.
Tail	Med. Dun Hackle Fibers.
Body	Muskrat Fur or Med. Gray Poly.
Hackle	Med. Dun.

Tri-Colour

Hook	Mustad 94838
Size	10 to 20
Thread	Brown
Body	Rear 1/3 - Light Dun Hackle.
	Middle 1/3 - Brown Hackle.
	Front 1/3 - Medium Dun Hackle.

Badger Spider

Hook	Mustad 94838
Size	10 to 14
Thread	Black
Tail	Badger Hackle Fibers.
Hackle	Badger at Least 2 Sizes Larger Than Normal.
Note	Furnace Spiders are also Quite Effective.

Hare's Ear Dry

Hook	Orvis 1509 or Orvis 1523.
Size	12 to 18.
Thread	Brown.
Tail	Brown Hackle Fibers or Guard Hairs.
Body	Hare's Mask Dubbing.
Rib	Fine Gold Mylar.
Hackle	Hare's Mask Guard Hairs Spun in a Loop and Wound as Hackle.

Fur Extended Body (March Brown)

Hook	Mustad 94838
Size	8 to 18
Thread	Tan
Wing	Speckled Hen Body Feather.
Tail	Natural Deer Hair
Body	Fawn Fox Fur or Poly.
Hackle	Brown and Grizzly Mixed.
Note	See Page 176 for Tying Instructions.

Adams Parachute

Hook	Orvis Premium or equivalent.
Size	10 to 18
Thread	Gray - 6/0 Pre-Waxed.
Wing	White Calf Tail Upright in a Single Clump.
Tail	Brown and Grizzly Hackle Fibers mixed.
Body	Muskrat Fur or Med. Gray Poly.
Hackle	Brown and Grizzly tied around Wing Base.

Light Cahill Parachute

Hook	Orvis Premium or equivalent.
Size	10 to 18
Thread	Cream - 6/0 Pre-Waxed.
Wing	White Calf Tail Upright in a Single Clump.
Tail	Dark Cream Hackle Fibers.
Body	Cream Fur or Poly.
Hackle	Dark Cream tied around Wing Base.

Black Gnat Parachute

Hook	Orvis Premium or equivalent.
Size	10 to 18
Thread	Black - 6/0 Pre-Waxed.
Wing	White Calf Tail Upright in a Single Clump.
Tail	Black Hackle Fibers.
Body	Black Fur or Poly.
Hackle	Black tied around Wing Base.

Royal Coachman Parachute

Hook	Orvis Premium or equivalent.
Size	10 to 18
Thread	Black - 6/0 Pre-Waxed.
Wing	White Calf Tail Upright in a Single Clump.
Tail	Golden Pheasant Tippet or Coachman Brown Hackle Fibers.
Body	Peacock Herl with a Red Floss Center Band.
Hackle	Coachman Brown tied around Wing Base.

Callibaetis Parachute

Hook	Orvis 1523 or Orvis 1509.
Size	14 to 18.
Thread	Gray.
Wing	Medium Dun Turkey Flat.
Tail	Grizzly Hackle Fibers.
Body	Tan/Olive Dubbing.
Hackle	Grizzly.

Parachute Mayfly

Hook	Orvis 1635.
Size	10 to 16.
Thread	Gray.
Wing	White Calf Tail and Body Hair.
Tail	Elk.
Body	Several Strands of Mottled Turkey Wound Around Hook.
Hackle	Grizzly.

Cut Wing Parachute (Adams)

Hook	Mustad 94840 or equivalent.
Size	10 to 20.
Thread	Gray
Wing	Grizzly Hen Body Feathers.
Tail	Cree Hackle Fibers.
Body	Muskrat Fur or Gray Poly.

Hare's Ear Parachute — Olive

Hook	Orvis 1635.
Size	10 to 16.
Thread	Olive.
Wing	White Calf Body Hair.
Tail	Olive Hare's Mask Guard Hairs.
Body	Olive Hare's Mask.
Rib	Olive Thread.
Hackle	Grizzly.

Green Drake Thorax

Hook	Orvis Supreme or equivalent.
Size	8 to 12
Thread	Tan - 6/0 Pre-Waxed.
Wing	Pale Brown Olive Turkey Flat.
Tail	Brown Hackle Fibers.
Body	Cream Fur or Poly.
Hackle	Light Bronze Dun and Grizzly mixed.

Brown Drake Thorax

Hook	Orvis Supreme or equivalent.
Size	8 to 12
Thread	Tan - 6/0 Pre-Waxed.
Wing	Medium Dun Turkey Flat.
Tail	Brown Hackle Fibers.
Body	Dirty Yellow (yellowish brown) Fur or Poly.
Hackle	Brown.

Pale Morning Dun Thorax

Hook	Orvis Supreme or equivalent.
Size	14 to 20
Thread	Yellow - 6/0 Pre-Waxed.
Wing	Light Dun Turkey Flat.
Tail	Light Dun Hackle Fibers.
Body	Pale Yellow Fur or Poly.
Hackle	Light Dun.

Blue Wing Olive Thorax

Hook	Orvis Supreme or equivalent.
Size	16 to 20
Thread	Olive - 6/0 Pre-Waxed.
Wing	Dark Dun Turkey Flat.
Tail	Medium Dun Hackle Fibers.
Body	Medium Olive Fur or Poly.
Hackle	Medium Dun.

Gray Fox Thorax

Hook	Orvis Supreme or equivalent.
Size	12 to 16
Thread	Yellow - 6/0 Pre-Waxed.
Wing	Light Dun Turkey Flat.
Tail	Golden Ginger Hackle Fibers.
Body	Pale Yellow Fur or Poly.
Hackle	Golden Ginger and Grizzly mixed.

March Brown Thorax

Hook	Orvis Supreme or equivalent.
Size	10 to 14
Thread	Tan - 6/0 Pre-Waxed.
Wing	Tan Turkey Flat.
Tail	Brown Hackle Fibers.
Body	Fawn Fox Fur or Poly.
Hackle	Brown and Grizzly mixed.

Red Quill Thorax

Hook	Orvis Supreme or equivalent.
Size	12 to 18
Thread	Tan - 6/0 Pre-Waxed.
Wing	Dark Dun Turkey Flat.
Tail	Bronze Dun Hackle Fibers.
Body	Mahogany Fur or Poly.
Hackle	Bronze Dun.

Quill Gordon Thorax

Hook	Orvis Supreme or equivalent.
Size	12 to 16
Thread	Yellow - 6/0 Pre-Waxed.
Wing	Dark Dun Turkey Flat.
Tail	Bronze Dun Hackle Fibers.
Body	Tan Fur or Poly.
Hackle	Bronze Dun.

Light Cahill Thorax

Hook	Orvis Supreme or equivalent.
Size	12 to 20
Thread	Yellow - 6/0 Pre-Waxed.
Wing	Cream Turkey Flat.
Tail	Dark Cream Hackle Fibers.
Body	Cream Fur or Poly.
Hackle	Dark Cream.

Hendrickson Thorax

Hook	Orvis Supreme or equivalent.
Size	12 to 16
Thread	Olive - 6/0 Pre-Waxed.
Wing	Medium Dun Turkey Flat.
Tail	Bronze Dun Hackle Fibers.
Body	Fawn Fox Fur or Poly.
Hackle	Bronze Dun.

Dark Blue Quill Thorax

Hook	Orvis Supreme or equivalent.
Size	16 to 20
Thread	Black - 6/0 Pre-Waxed.
Wing	Dark Dun Turkey Flat.
Tail	Dark Dun Hackle Fibers.
Body	Chocolate Brown Fur or Poly.
Hackle	Dark Dun.

Iron Blue Dun Thorax

Hook	Orvis Supreme or equivalent.
Size	16 to 20
Thread	Tan - 6/0 Pre-Waxed.
Wing	Dark Dun Turkey Flat.
Tail	Dark Dun Hackle Fibers.
Body	Mahogany Fur or Poly.
Hackle	Dark Dun.

Adams Thorax

Hook	Mustad 94840
Size	10 to 20
Thread	Gray
Wing	Teal Flank Feather.
Tail	Brown Hackle Fibers.
Hackle	Brown and Grizzly Mixed.
Body	Gray Poly.

Brown Thorax

Hook	Mustad 94840
Size	10 to 20
Thread	Brown
Wing	White Turkey Flat.
Tail	Brown Hackle Fibers.
Hackle	Brown
Body	Reddish Brown Poly.

Loop Wing Extended Body Dun

Hook	Orvis 1523 or Orvis 1509.
Size	12 to 18.
Thread	To Match Body Color.
Wing	Wood Duck Tied Loop Style.
Tail	Microfibetts Tied Long.
Body	Fine Cream Dubbing Wound Over Butts of Tail then on to Hook.
Hackle	Ginger Clipped Flat on Bottom.
Note:	This pattern tied as a Blue Wing Olive works well.

Cut Wing Thorax (March Brown)

Hook	Mustad 94840 or equivalent.
Size	10 to 20.
Thread	Tan
Wing	Speckled Hen Body Feather.
Tail	Cree Hackle Fibers.
Body	Fawn Fox Fur or Poly.
Hackle	Brown and Grizzly Mixed.
Note	See Back of Page 6 for additional Patterns.

Speckled Spinner

Hook	Orvis Supreme or equivalent.
Size	14 to 18
Thread	Yellow - 6/0 Pre-Waxed.
Wing	Light Gray Polywing Material with a Black Polywing Material leading edge.
Tail	Dark Cream Hackle Fibers.
Body	Fawn Fox Fur or Poly.

Pale Olive Spinner

Hook	Orvis Supreme or equivalent.
Size	14 to 20
Thread	Olive - 6/0 Pre-Waxed.
Wing	Light Gray Polywing Material.
Tail	Light Dun Hackle Fibers.
Body	Pale Olive Fur or Poly.

Black-White Spinner

Hook	Orvis Supreme or equivalent.
Size	20 to 26
Thread	Black - 6/0 Pre-Waxed.
Wing	Light Gray Polywing Material.
Tail	Light Dun Hackle Fibers.
Body	Black Fur or Poly.

Caenis Spinner

Hook	Orvis Supreme or equivalent.
Size	20 to 26
Thread	Black - 6/0 Pre-Waxed.
Wing	Light Gray Polywing Material.
Tail	Light Dun Hackle Fibers.
Abdomen	White Thread
Thorax	Gray Fur or Poly.

Green Drake Spinner

Hook	Orvis Supreme or equivalent.
Size	10 and 12
Thread	Yellow - 6/0 Pre-Waxed.
Wing	Light Gray Polywing Material.
Tail	Dark Cream Hackle Fibers.
Body	Cream Fur or Poly.

Brown Drake Spinner

Hook	Orvis Supreme or equivalent.
Size	10 and 12
Thread	Tan - 6/0 Pre-Waxed.
Wing	Light Gray Polywing Material.
Tail	Brown Hackle Fibers.
Body	Dirty Yellow (yellowish brown) Fur or Poly.
Rib	Brown Floss.

Rusty Spinner

Hook	Orvis Supreme or equivalent.
Size	12 to 24
Thread	Tan - 6/0 Pre-Waxed.
Wing	Light Gray Polywing Material.
Tail	Medium Dun Hackle Fibers.
Body	Rusty Brown (fiery brown) Fur or Poly.

Pale Sulphur Spinner

Hook	Orvis Supreme or equivalent.
Size	14 to 18
Thread	Yellow - 6/0 Pre-Waxed.
Wing	Light Gray Polywing Material.
Tail	Light Dun Hackle Fibers.
Body	Creamy Orange (salmon) Fur or Poly.

Hackle Spinner (Typical)

Hook	Mustad 94840 or Equivalent.
Size	10 to 24
Thread	Color to Complement Body
Tail	Light Dun Hackle Fibers - Divided
Wing	Light Dun Hackle Wound and Clipped on Top and Bottom.
Body	Poly Dubbing - The Body can be any Color to Imitate the Naturals in Your Area. See page 193 for additional patterns.

Hen Wing Spinner

Hook	Mustad 94840 or Equivalent.
Size	10 to 24
Thread	Color to Complement Body
Tail	Light Dun Hackle Fibers - Divided
Wing	Light Dun Hen Hackle Tips
Body	Poly Dubbing - The Body can be any Color to Imitate the Naturals in Your Area. See page 193 for additional patterns.

Sparkle Spinner

Hook	Orvis 1637 or Orvis 1523.
Size	12 to 20.
Thread	To Match Body Color.
Wing	Magic Wing.
Tail	Hackle Fibers Tied Split.
Body	Fine Dubbing.
Note	Can be tied in any color to match local spinner falls.

Hair Extended Body (Spinner)

Hook	Mustad 94838
Size	8 to 18
Thread	Brown
Abdomen	Deer, Body Hair Dyed Dark Brown Tied Parallel to Hook Shank.
Tail	Same as Abdomen.
Wing	Blue Dun Body Feather.
Thorax	Dark Brown Poly Dubbing.
Note	See Page 175 for Tying Instructions.

Gray - Olive

Hook   Orvis Premium or equivalent.
Size   20 to 24
Thread   Olive - 6/0 Pre-Waxed.
Tail   Light Dun Hackle Fibers - Divided.
Wing   Light Mallard Wing Quill Segments - Upright and Divided.
Body   Pale Olive Fur or Poly.

Gray - Yellow

Hook   Orvis Premium or equivalent.
Size   16 to 20
Thread   Yellow - 6/0 Pre-Waxed.
Tail   Light Dun Hackle Fibers - Divided.
Wing   Light Mallard Wing Quill Segments - Upright and Divided.
Body   Pale Yellow Fur or Poly.

Slate - Olive

Hook   Orvis Premium or equivalent.
Size   16 and 18
Thread   Olive - 6/0 Pre-Waxed.
Tail   Medium Dun Hackle Fibers - Divided.
Wing   Dark Mallard Wing Quill Segments - Upright and Divided.
Body   Pale Olive Fur or Poly.

White - Black

Hook   Orvis Premium or equivalent.
Size   20 to 26
Thread   Black - 6/0 Pre-Waxed.
Tail   Light Dun Hackle Fibers - Divided.
Wing   White Duck Wing Quill Segments - Upright and Divided.
Body   Black Fur or Poly.

Sparkle Dun

Hook	Orvis 1637 or Orvis 1523.
Size	10 to 20.
Thread	To Match Body Color.
Wing	Deer Body Hair Tied Fan Shape. See Page 4 of Index Supplement I for Tying Instructions.
Tail	Magic Wing or Antron® Yarn.
Body	Fine Dubbing.
Note:	Can be tied in any color to match local hatches.

Haystack

Hook	Mustad 94840
Size	8 to 18
Thread	Tan
Wing	Light Tan Elk or Deer Hair.
Tail	Light Tan Elk or Deer Hair.
Body	Amber Fur or Poly
Note	See Page 167 for Tying Instructions and additional patterns.

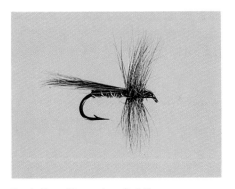

Dark Dun Fluttering Caddis

Hook   Orvis Premium or equivalent.
Size   14 to 18
Thread   Black - 6/0 Pre-Waxed.
Rib   Fine Gold Wire.
Body   Mahogany Ringneck Pheasant Center Tail Fibers.
Wing   Dark Dun Hackle Fibers or Mink Tail Guard Hairs.
Hackle   Dark Dun.

Light Dun Fluttering Caddis

Hook   Orvis Premium or equivalent.
Size   14 to 18
Thread   Gray - 6/0 Pre-Waxed.
Rib   Fine Gold Wire.
Body   Mahogany Ringneck Pheasant Center Tail Fibers.
Wing   Light Dun Hackle Fibers or Mink Tail Guard Hairs.
Hackle   Light Dun.

Light Shad Fluttering Caddis

Hook   Orvis Premium or equivalent.
Size   14 to 18
Thread   Black - 6/0 Pre-Waxed.
Rib   Fine Gold Wire.
Body   Mahogany Ringneck Pheasant Center Tail Fibers.
Wing   Med. Dun and Ginger Hackle Fibers mixed or Mink Tail Guard Hairs.
Hackle   Ginger and Grizzly mixed.

Small Brown Fluttering Caddis

Hook   Orvis Premium or equivalent.
Size   16 to 20
Thread   Tan - 6/0 Pre-Waxed.
Rib   Fine Gold Wire.
Body   Mahogany Ringneck Pheasant Center Tail Fibers.
Wing   Brown Hackle Fibers or Mink Tail Guard Hairs.
Hackle   Brown.

Large Ginger Fluttering Caddis

Hook   Orvis Premium or equivalent.
Size   12 and 14
Thread Tan - 6/0 Pre-Waxed.
Rib   Fine Gold Wire.
Body   Mahogany Ringneck Pheasant
        Center Tail Fibers.
Wing   Ginger Hackle Fibers or Mink
        Tail Guard Hairs.
Hackle Ginger.

Large Red Fluttering Caddis

Hook   Orvis Premium or equivalent.
Size   12 and 14
Thread Tan - 6/0 Pre-Waxed.
Rib   Fine Gold Wire.
Body   Mahogany Ringneck Pheasant
        Center Tail Fibers.
Wing   Brown Hackle Fibers or Mink
        Tail Guard Hairs.
Hackle Brown.

Gray Tent Wing Caddis

Hook   Orvis Premium or equivalent.
Size   12 to 20
Thread Black - 6/0 Pre-Waxed.
Body   Muskrat or Dark Dun Poly.
Hackle Light Dun - Clipped top and bottom.
Wing   Mallard Wing Quill Segment.

Brown Tent Wing Caddis

Hook   Orvis Premium or equivalent.
Size   12 to 20
Thread Black - 6/0 Pre-Waxed.
Body   Mahogany Ringneck Pheasant
        Center Tail Fibers.
Hackle Dark Ginger - Clipped top and
        bottom.
Wing   Oak Turkey Wing Quill Segment.

Goddard Caddis

Hook   Mustad 9671
Size   10 to 16
Thread   Green
Body   Deer Hair Spun and Clipped to
          Shape in any Color.
Hackle   Brown, Dun or Grizzly.
Antennae Brown Hackle Quills.

Stillborn Elk Caddis

Hook   Orvis 1523 or Orvis 1635.
Size   12 to 20.
Thread To Match Body Color.
Body   Antron Dubbing.
Wing   Elk Body or Hock Hair.
Head   Fur Dubbing.
Note   Can be tied in any color to match
        local Caddis Hatches.

Rick's Magic Wing Caddis

Hook   Orvis 1635.
Size   10 to 16.
Thread Gray.
Body   Olive Dubbing Palmered with Dun
        Hackle and Clipped.
Wing   Magic Wing or Organza Burned to
        Shape with a Wing Burner.
Note   Organza is available in local fabric
        shops.

Rick's Tan Caddis

Hook   Orvis 1635.
Size   12 to 18.
Thread To Match Body Color.
Body   Tan Dubbing Palmed with Brown
        and Grizzly Hackle Clipped.
Wing   Traun Sedge Wing.
Hackle Brown and Grizzly.

Delta Wing Caddis

Hook	Mustad 94833 or 94840
Size	10 to 20
Thread	Brown
Body	Olive Fur or Poly.
Wing	Brown Hackle Tips Tied on Each Side of Hook - Slanted Back at 45° Angle from the Hook Shank.
Hackle	Brown
Note	See Page 193 for additional patterns.

Elk Wing Caddis

Hook	Mustad 94833 or 94840
Size	10 to 20
Thread	Brown
Body	Olive Fur or Poly.
Hackle	Brown Palmed over Body.
Wing	Light Elk Hair Tied on Top of the Hook Allowing Several Fibers to Extend Along Sides. The Wing Butts should extend Forward to Form Head.
Note	See Page 193 for additional patterns.

Chuck Caddis (Modified)

Hook	Mustad 94838 or Partridge Sedge
Size	10 to 18
Thread	Tan
Body	1/2 English Hare's Ear and 1/2 Australian Opposum Mixed.
Wing	Woodchuck Guard Hairs.
Hackle	Brown and Grizzly Mixed.

Vermont Hare's Ear

Hook	Mustad 94838
Size	10 to 18
Thread	Tan
Body	1/2 English Hare's Ear and 1/2 Australian Opossum Mixed - Tied Down Around Bend.
Hackle	Brown and Grizzly Mixed Hackle. Should be Tied Full and Clipped.
Note	Fly Works Best When Skated.

Kaufmann's Stimulator

Hook	Orvis 1638.
Size	10 to 16.
Thread	Fire Orange.
Tail	Elk Body Hair.
Body	Rust Dubbing Palmed with Brown Hackle.
Wing	Elk Body Hair.
Head	Golden Yellow Dubbing.
Hackle	Grizzly Palmed thru Head.

Dancing Caddis

Hook	Partridge Swedish Dry Fly.
Size	10 to 16
Thread	Black
Body	Sparse Dubbing - Color to Duplicate Desired Caddis Pattern.
Wing	Deer Hair - Color to Duplicate Desired Caddis Pattern.
Hackle	Color to Duplicate Desired Caddis Pattern.

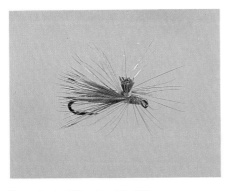

Parachute Elkwing Caddis

Hook	Orvis 1509 or Orvis 1635.
Size	12 to 18.
Thread	To Match Body Color.
Body	Tan Dubbing.
Wing	Natural Elk Body or Hock Hair.
Hackle	Ginger Wound Parachute Style Around Wing Butt.
Note	This pattern can be tied in any combination of colors to match natural insects in your area.

Parachute Caddis

Hook	Orvis 1635.
Size	10 to 16.
Thread	Gray.
Upright Wing	White Calf Body Hair.
Down Wing	Mottled Turkey Quill.
Body	Hare's Mask.
Hackle	Grizzly.

Henryville Special

Hook	Orvis Premium or equivalent.
Size	12 to 20
Thread	Olive - 6/0 Pre-Waxed.
Rib	Grizzly Hackle Palmered in Open Spiral.
Body	Light Olive Floss.
Wing	Bunch of Lemon Wood Duck over which a pair of Mallard Wing Quill Segments are Tied Downwing.
Hackle	Dark Ginger.

King's River Caddis

Hook	Orvis Premium or equivalent.
Size	12 to 20
Thread	Black - 6/0 Pre-Waxed.
Body	Tan to Light Brown Fur or Poly.
Wing	Oak Mottled Turkey Wing Segment Tied Downwing.
Hackle	Brown.

Terrestrials

Grasshopper

Hook	Mustad 9672
Size	8 to 12
Thread	Yellow
Tail	Red Bucktail.
Body	Amber Transluscent Dubbing.
Rib	Brown Saddle Hackle Clipped.
Under Wing	Several Strands of the Brown Part of a Yellow Bucktail.
Wing	Turkey Wing Quill Segment.
Legs	Golden or Ringneck Tail Quill Segments.
Head	Golden Brown Deer Body Hair, Spun and Clipped to Shape.
Note	See Page 172 for Tying Instructions.

Paradrake — Green Drake

Hook	Orvis 1637 or Orvis 1509.
Size	8 to 16.
Thread	To Match Body Color.
Wing	Moose Body Hair.
Body	Olive Deer Body Hair Tied in Forward and Pulled Back and Overwrapped with Tying Thread.
Tail	Moose Body Hair.
Hackle	Grizzly Dyed Yellow.
Note	This pattern can be tied in any combination of colors to match naturals in your area.

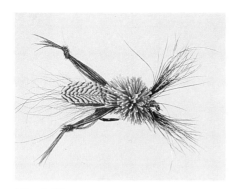

Bing's Hopper

Hook	Orvis 1638 or Orvis 1640.
Size	8 to 14.
Thread	Tan.
Body	Tan Dubbing.
Rib	Fine Gold Mylar Tinsel.
Rear Legs	Knotted Ringneck Pheasant Tail Fibers.
Wing	Wood Duck.
Head	Spun Antelope Body Hair.
Front Legs	Elk Body Hair.

Henry's Fork Hopper

Hook	Orvis 1638 or Orvis 1640.
Size	8 to 14.
Thread	Yellow.
Body	White Deer Body Hair Tied in with Tips Toward Hook Bend Then Pulled Forward to Head.
Rib	Yellow Thread.
Wing	Speckled Hen Saddle Feather, Lacquered and Tied Over Body.
Head	Elk Body Hair Tied Forward Then Pulled Back to Form Head and Collar.

Parachute Hopper

Hook	Orvis 1638 or Orvis 1640.
Size	8 to 14.
Thread	Pale Yellow.
Upright Wing	White Calf Body Hair.
Body	Golden Brown Antron® Dubbing.
Down Wing	Mottled Turkey Quill.
Legs	Knotted Ringneck Pheasant Tail Fibers.
Hackle	Grizzly.

Cricket

Hook	Orvis 1638 or Orvis 1640.
Size	8 to 14.
Thread	Black.
Tail	Moose Body Hair.
Body	Brown Dubbing with Black Palmered Hackle Rib; Clipped.
Legs	Black Hackle Quills; Knotted.
Head/ Collar	Black Deer Body Hair.

Black Ant

Hook	Orvis Premium or equivalent.
Size	14 to 24
Thread	Black - 6/0 Pre-Waxed.
Body	Black Fur or Poly.
Hackle	Black.

Cinnamon Ant

Hook	Orvis Premium or equivalent.
Size	18 to 24
Thread	Tan - 6/0 Pre-Waxed.
Body	Cinnamon Brown Fur or Poly.
Hackle	Dark Ginger.

Letort Cricket

Hook	Mustad 94831 or 9671.
Size	8 to 16
Thread	Black - Pre-Waxed Monocord.
Body	Black Fur or Poly.
Wing	Single Black Goose Wing Quill Segment cut to shape, lacquered and tied flat over body.
Head	Spun Black Deer Body Hair clipped to shape.

Letort Hopper

Hook	Mustad 94831 or 9671.
Size	8 to 16
Thread	Yellow - Pre-Waxed Monocord.
Body	Yellow Fur or Poly.
Wing	Single Oak Turkey Wing Quill Segment cut to shape, lacquered and tied flat over body.
Head	Spun Natural Gray Deer Body Hair clipped to shape.

Red Flying Ant

Hook	Orvis Premium or equivalent
Size	14 to 18
Thread	Black - 6/0 Pre-Waxed.
Aft Body	Red Wintuk Orlon No. 140.
Tail	Moose Body Hair.
Wing	Mallard Wing Quill Segment.
Hackle	Black.
Fore-Body	Red Wintuk Orlon.

Black Flying Ant

Hook	Orvis Premium or equivalent.
Size	14 to 18
Thread	Black - 6/0 Pre-Waxed.
Aft Body	Black Wintuk Orlon No. 140.
Tail	Moose Body Hair
Wing	Mallard Wing Quill Segment.
Hackle	Black.
Fore-Body	Black Wintuk Orlon.

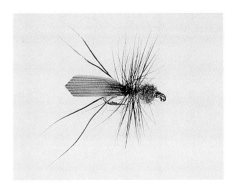

Brown Flying Ant

Hook	Orvis Premium or equivalent.
Size	14 to 18
Thread	Black - 6/0 Pre-Waxed.
Aft Body	Dark Brown Wintuk Orlon No. 140.
Tail	Moose Body Hair.
Wing	Mallard Wing Quill Segment.
Hackle	Black
Fore-Body	Dark Brown Wintuk Orlon.

Deer Hopper

Hook	Mustad 9672 or 94831.
Size	6 to 14
Thread	Yellow - Pre-Waxed Monocord.
Tail	Red Hackle Fibers.
Body	Spun Yellow Deer Body Hair clipped to shape.
Wing	Oak Mottled Turkey or equivalent.
Hackle	Brown and Grizzly mixed.

McMurrey Beetle

Hook	Orvis 1637.
Size	14 to 20.
Thread	To Match Body Color.
Tail	Brown or Black Bucktail Hair.
Aft Body	McMurrey Emerger Body - Paint Brown or Black.
Head/Wing	Brown or Black Deer Body Hair. Tied Forward and Pulled Back. Clip to Desired Length.

Ethafoam Ant

Hook	Orvis 1637.
Size	14 to 20.
Thread	To Match Body Color.
Legs	3 or 4 Strands of Deer Body Hair.
Body	Ethafoam Cut to Shape and Tied in on Top of Hook to Produce Body Segments - Color with Waterproof Marker.

McMurrey Ant

Hook	Orvis 1637.
Size	14 to 20.
Thread	To Match Body Color.
Body	McMurrey Ant Body - Paint Desired Color.
Hackle	To Match Body Color.

Visible Beetle

Hook	Orvis 1635 or Orvis 1637
Size	14 to 20.
Thread	To Match Body Color.
Body	Peacock Herl.
Back/Legs	Black Deer Body Hair Pulled Over Body and Tied in at Eye. Clip to Form Head and Legs.
Wing	Elk Body Hair.

Black Beetle

Hook	Orvis Premium or equivalent.
Size	14 to 20
Thread	Black - 6/0 Pre-Waxed.
Wing	Gray Goose Wing Segment tied in at bend and pulled over body.
Hackle	Black Palmered through body and clipped flat on the bottom.
Body	Peacock Herl.

Black Crowe Beetle

Hook	Orvis Premium or equivalent.
Size	14 to 20
Thread	Black - 6/0 Pre-Waxed.
Body	Black Deer Body Hair.
Legs	Black Deer Body Hair.

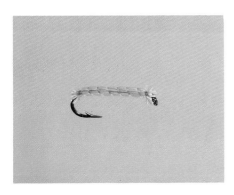

Inch Worm

Hook	Orvis Supreme or equivalent.
Size	12 to 16
Thread	Yellow - 6/0 Pre-Waxed.
Rib	Insect Green Floss - Single strand of Four Strand Floss.
Body	Insect Green Deer Body Hair tied parallel to the hook shank.

Green Leaf Hopper

Hook	Orvis Premium or equivalent.
Size	16 to 22
Thread	White - 6/0 Pre-Waxed.
Body	White Thread.
Hackle	Insect Green Hackle Palmered over body - clipped flat on top and bottom.
Wing	Insect Green Mallard or Wood Duck Breast Feather lacquered cut to shape and tied flat over body.

Ausable Wulff

Hook	Mustad 94840 or equivalent.
Size	8 to 14
Thread	Red - 6/0 Pre-Waxed.
Wing	White Calf Tail - Upright and Divided.
Tail	Woodchuck Tail Fibers or Moose Body Hair.
Body	Bleached Australian Opossum.
Hackle	Brown and Grizzly mixed.

Hairwing Royal Coachman

Hook	Mustad 94840 or equivalent.
Size	8 to 14
Thread	Black - 6/0 Pre-Waxed.
Wing	White Calf Tail - Upright and Divided.
Tail	White Calf Tail or Mink Tail Guard Hairs.
Body	Peacock Herl with Red Floss Center Joint.
Hackle	Brown.

Royal Wulff

Hook	Mustad 94840 or equivalent.
Size	8 to 14
Thread	Black - 6/0 Pre-Waxed.
Wing	White Calf Tail - Upright and Divided.
Tail	Natural Deer Body Hair Tips or Moose Body Hair.
Body	Peacock Herl with Red Floss Center Band.
Hackle	Brown.

Royal Coachman (Trude)

Hook	Mustad 94840
Size	8 to 16
Thread	Black
Tail	Golden Pheasant Tippet
Body	Peacock Herl with a Red Floss Center Band.
Wing	White Calf Tail.
Hackle	Coachman Brown.

White Wulff

Hook	Mustad 94840 or equivalent.
Size	8 to 14
Thread	White - 6/0 Pre-Waxed.
Wing	White Calf Tail - Upright and Divided.
Tail	White Calf Tail or Mink Tail Guard Hairs.
Body	White Fur or Poly.
Hackle	Badger.

Gray Wulff

Hook	Mustad 94840 or equivalent.
Size	8 to 14
Thread	Black - 6/0 Pre-Waxed.
Wing	Natural Deer Body Hair - Upright and Divided.
Tail	Natural Deer Body Hair Tips or Moose Body Hair.
Body	Muskrat or Medium Gray Poly.
Hackle	Medium Dun.

Grizzly Wulff

Hook	Mustad 94840 or equivalent.
Size	8 to 14
Thread	Black - 6/0 Pre-Waxed.
Wing	Natural Deer Body Hair - Upright and Divided.
Tail	Natural Deer Body Hair Tips or Med. Gray Mink Tail Guard Hair.
Body	Yellow Floss or Poly.
Hackle	Brown and Grizzly mixed.

Green Drake Wulff

Hook	Mustad 94840
Size	10 to 16
Thread	Brown
Wing	Sable or Moose Body Hair.
Tail	Moose Body Hair.
Body	Olive Poly.
Rib	Light Olive Floss.
Hackle	Yellow Dyed Grizzly.

Adams Irresistible

Hook	Mustad 94840 or equivalent.
Size	8 to 14
Thread	Black - Pre-Waxed Monocord.
Tail	Brown Hackle Fibers or Mink Tail Guard Hairs.
Body	Spun Gray Deer Hair Clipped to Shape.
Wing	Grizzly Hackle Tips - Upright and Divided.
Hackle	Brown and Grizzly mixed.

White Irresistible

Hook	Mustad 94840 or equivalent.
Size	8 to 14
Thread	White - Pre-Waxed Monocord.
Tail	White Hackle Fibers or Mink Tail Guard Hairs.
Body	Spun White Deer Hair Clipped to Shape.
Wing	Badger Hackle Tips - Upright and Divided.
Hackle	Badger.

Humpy

Hook	Mustad 94840 or equivalent.
Size	8 to 14
Thread	Red or Yellow - Pre-Waxed Monocord
Tail	Moose Body Hair
Body	Natural Deer Hair pulled over Thread Underbody.
Wing	Formed from the Tips of the Deer Hair used to make the body.
Hackle	Grizzly.

Rat Faced McDougal

Hook	Mustad 94840 or equivalent.
Size	8 to 14
Thread	White - Pre-Waxed Monocord.
Tail	Dark Ginger Hackle Fibers or Mink Tail Guard Hairs.
Body	Spun Light Gray Deer Hair Clipped to Shape.
Wing	Dark Ginger Variant Hackle Tips - Upright and Divided.
Hackle	Dark Ginger.

Renegade

Hook	Mustad 94840
Size	8 to 18
Thread	Black
Rear	
Hackle	Brown
Tag	Gold Tinsel
Body	Peacock Herl.
Front	
Hackle	Cream or White.

H and L Variant

Hook	Mustad 94840
Size	10 to 16
Thread	Black
Wing	White Calftail - Upright and Divided.
Tail	White Calftail.
Body	1/2 Stripped Peacock - Front 1/2 Peacock Herl.
Hackle	Furnace.

Light Spruce

Hook	Mustad 94840
Size	10 to 18
Thread	Black
Wing	Badger Hackle Tips Tied Up-Right and Divided.
Tail	Dark Moose Hair
Body	1/2 Red Floss - Front 1/2 Peacock Herl.
Hackle	Badger.

Waterwalker (Typical)

Hook	Mustad 94840
Size	10 to 16
Thread	Color to Complement Body.
Wings	Elk or Deer Hair Upright and Divided.
Tail	Deer Elk or Moose Hair.
Body	Poly Dubbing.
Hackle	Tied Waterwalker (Style).
Note	See Page 168 for Tying Instructions.

Golden Stone

Hook	Mustad 9672
Size	4 to 10
Thread	Black
Tail	Light Elk.
Body	Yellow Poly Ribbed with a Palmered Ginger Hackle.
Wing	Light Elk.
Hackle	Ginger Tied Full.

Improved Sofa Pillow

Hook	Mustad 9672
Size	4 to 10
Thread	Black
Tail	Natural Elk.
Body	Burnt Orange Poly Ribbed with a Palmered Brown Hackle.
Wing	Natural Elk.
Hackle	Brown Tied Full.

Henry's Fork Salmon Fly

Hook	Mustad 9672
Size	4 to 10
Thread	Orange
Tail	Moose Body.
Body	Light Orange Poly Ribbed with a Palmered Dun Hackle.
Wing	Elk
Head	Moose Body Hair Tied Forward Then Pulled Back to Form Bullet Shaped Head.

Hair Spider

Hook	Mustad 94838
Size	10 to 16
Thread	Brown
Legs	2 Clumps of Deer Hair Spun on the Hook Opposing each other then Pushed Together to Form a Single Clump.

Trico Parachute

Hook   Orvis 1637.
Size   18 to 24.
Thread   Black.
Wing   White Turkey Flat.
Tail   Light Dun Hackle Fibers.
Abdomen   Black Tying Thread.
Thorax   Fine Black Dubbing.
Hackle   Light Dun.

Trico Spinner

Hook   Orvis 1637.
Size   18 to 24.
Thread   Black.
Wing   Light Dun Hackle Fibers.
Tail   Light Dun Hackle Fibers.
Abdomen   Black Tying Thread.
Thorax   Fine Black Dubbing.

Griffith's Gnat

Hook   Orvis 1637.
Size   16 to 22.
Thread   Black.
Body   Peacock Herl.
Hackle   Grizzly Palmed thru Body.

Midge Nymph

Hook   Orvis 1637.
Size   18 to 24.
Thread   To Match Head Color.
Abdomen   Stripped Hackle Quill wound around
          hook.
Thorax   Hare's Ear Dubbing.
Note: Can be tied in any color
          combination.

Adams

Hook	Orvis Premium or equivalent.
Size	20 to 28
Thread	Black - 6/0 Pre-Waxed.
Tail	Brown and Grizzly Hackle Fibers mixed.
Body	Muskrat Fur or Dark Dun Poly.
Hackle	Brown and Grizzly Mixed.

Cream

Hook	Orvis Premium or equivalent.
Size	20 to 28
Thread	Cream - 6/0 Pre-Waxed.
Tail	Dark Cream Hackle Fibers.
Body	Cream Fur or Poly.
Hackle	Dark Cream.

Brown

Hook	Orvis Premium or equivalent.
Size	20 to 28
Thread	Gray - 6/0 Pre-Waxed.
Tail	Brown Hackle Fibers.
Body	Medium Brown Fur or Poly.
Hackle	Brown.

Black

Hook	Orvis Premium or equivalent.
Size	20 to 28
Thread	Black - 6/0 Pre-Waxed.
Tail	Black Hackle Fibers.
Body	Black Fur or Poly.
Hackle	Black.

Iwamasa Dun - March Brown

Hook	Mustad 94840 or Equivalent.
Size	12 to 16
Thread	Tan
Legs	Medium Dun Hackle Fibers.
Tail	Medium Dun Hackle Fibers.
Body	Tan Fur or Poly.
Wing	Hungarian Partridge - Cut or Burned to Shape.

Iwamasa Dun - Hendrickson

Hook	Mustad 94840 or Equivalent.
Size	12 to 16
Thread	Tan
Legs	Light Elk Hair.
Tail	Medium Dun Hackle Fibers.
Body	Reddish Brown Poly with Reddish Brown Elk Hair Pulled Over Back and Ribbed with Black Thread.
Wing	Dark Dun Hen - Cut or Burned to Shape.

Iwamasa Spinner - Trico

Hook	Mustad 94840 or 94859
Size	20 to 26
Thread	Black
Tail	Light Dun Hackle Fibers.
Wing	White Hen - Cut or Burned to Shape.
Body	Black Poly.

Iwamasa Spinner - Rusty

Hook	Mustad 94840
Size	12 to 20
Thread	Tan
Tail	Light Dun Hackle Fibers.
Wing	White Hen - Cut or Burned to Shape.
Body	Reddish Brown Poly with Reddish Brown Elk Hair Pulled Over Back and Ribbed with Orange Thread.

Loop Wing Dun

Hook	Mustad 94838
Size	10 to 18
Thread	Gray
Tail	Gray Squirrel Tail.
Legs	Gray Squirrel Tail.
Wing	Teal Flank Fibers.
Body	Gray Fur or Poly.

Poly Wing Dun

Hook	Mustad 94838
Size	10 to 18
Thread	White
Legs	Microfibetts
Body	Polypropylene Yarn.
Tail	Microfibetts
Wing	Polyethylene Cut to Shape.
Note	See Page 173 for Tying Instructions.

A multitude of patterns may be obtained by tinting various fly parts with waterproof marking pens.

Poly Spinner

Hook	Mustad 94838
Size	8 to 18
Thread	White
Wing	Microfibetts
Body	Polypropylene Yarn.
Tail	Microfibetts

Poly Nymph

Hook	Mustad 94838
Size	8 to 20
Thread	White
Tail	Microfibetts
Body & Legs	Polypropylene Yarn.
Wing Case	Polypropylene Yarn.
Note:	A multitude of patterns may be obtained by tinting the various fly parts with waterproof marking pens.

Mayfly Emerger

Hook   Mustad 94840
Size   12 to 20
Thread   Color to Match Body.
Tail   Wood Duck Fibers.
Abdomen   Poly Dubbing.
Rib   Fine Gold Wire.
Wings   Mallard Quill Segments Tied on
           Sides.
Thorax   Poly Dubbing.
Note: Fly may be tied in any color
           to suit your need. Olive, Black
           and Yellow are the most popular.

Chironomid Pupa

Hook   Mustad 94840
Size   14 to 20
Thread   Black
Tail   White Rabbit Fur.
Body   Olive, Black, Gray, Yellow or
           Brown Dubbing.
Rib   Fine Copper Wire.
Head   Black Dubbing.
Breathing White Rabbit Fur.
Filaments

Mosquito Emerger

Hook   Mustad 94840
Size   14 to 20
Thread   Black.
Tail   Grizzly Hackle Fibers.
Abdomen   Stripped Peacock Quill.
Thorax   Peacock Herl.
Wings   Grizzly Hackle Tips Tied Short.

Chironomid Emerger

Hook   Mustad 94840
Size   14 to 20
Thread   Black
Tail   White Rabbit Fur.·
Abdomen   Black, Olive, Gray, Yellow or
           Brown Dubbing.
Rib   Fine Silver Wire.
Head   Black Dubbing.
Wings   Grizzly Hackle Tips.
Antennae   Grizzly Hackle Fibers.

Chironomid

Hook	Orvis 1524.
Size	12 to 18.
Thread	Gray.
Tail	White Marabou.
Body	Mottled Turkey Quill Fibers.
Rib	Gold Wire.
Head	Peacock Herl.
Air Sac	White Marabou.

Elk Wing Emerger

Hook	Orvis 1510.
Size	12 to 20.
Thread	To Match Body Color.
Tail	Ringneck Pheasant Tail Fibers.
Body	Tan Antron® Dubbing.
Rib	Brown Thread.
Wing Case	Elk Body Hair Tied in to Extend Past Eye.
Head	Tan Antron Dubbing.
Note:	Also effective in other body colors such as olive.

Harrop Surface Emerger

Hook	Orvis 1509 or Orvis 1523.
Size	12 to 20.
Thread	Cream.
Tail	Wood Duck.
Body	Cream Dubbing.
Wing	Duck Quill Fibers, Clipped.
Legs	Partridge Hackle or Speckled Hen Saddle Fibers.
Head	Cream Dubbing.
Note:	Also effective in other colors such as rust.

Balsa Emerger

Hook	Orvis 1637.
Size	12 to 20.
Thread	Olive.
Tail	Ringneck Pheasant Tail Fibers.
Body	Olive Antron® Dubbing.
Wing	Dun Turkey Flat.
Legs	Speckled Hen Saddle Fibers.
Air Sac	Orvis Balsa Emerger Body.
Note:	Also effective in other color combinations to match local hatches.

Brown

Hook	Orvis Premium or equivalent.
Size	12 to 20
Thread	Brown - 6/0 Pre-Waxed.
Tail	Brown Hackle Fibers.
Rib	Brown Silk or Floss.
Abdomen	Light Brown Poly.
Wing Case	Dark Brown Poly.
Legs	Brown Hackle Fibers.
Thorax	Brown Poly.

Cream

Hook	Orvis Premium or equivalent.
Size	12 to 20
Thread	Cream - 6/0 Pre-Waxed.
Tail	Dark Cream Hackle Fibers.
Rib	Yellow Silk or Floss.
Abdomen	Cahill Cream Poly.
Wing Case	Amber Poly.
Legs	Dark Cream Hackle Fibers.
Thorax	Cahill Cream Poly (same as abdomen).

Olive

Hook	Orvis Premium or equivalent.
Size	12 to 20
Thread	Olive - 6/0 Pre-Waxed.
Tail	Dark Dun Hackle Fibers.
Rib	Yellow Silk or Floss.
Abdomen	Bronze Olive Poly.
Wing Case	Dark Dun Poly.
Legs	Dark Dun Hackle Fibers.
Thorax	Bronze Olive Poly (same as abdomen).

Yellow

Hook	Orvis Premium or equivalent.
Size	12 to 20
Thread	Yellow - 6/0 Pre-Waxed.
Tail	Cream Hackle Fibers.
Rib	Olive Silk or Floss.
Abdomen	Primrose Poly.
Wing Case	Light Dun Poly.
Legs	Cream Hackle Fibers.
Thorax	Primrose Poly (same as abdomen).

Brown Wooly Worm

Hook	Mustad 9672 or equivalent.
Size	6 to 12
Thread	Black - 6/0 Pre-Waxed.
Tail	Red Hackle Fibers.
Hackle	Furnace Palmered over body.
Body	Brown Chenille.

Black Wooly Worm

Hook	Mustad 9672 or equivalent.
Size	6 to 12
Thread	Black - 6/0 Pre-Waxed.
Tail	Red Hackle Fibers.
Hackle	Badger Palmered over body.
Body	Black Chenille.

Picket Pin

Hook	Mustad 9672 or equivalent.
Size	8 to 12
Thread	Black - 6/0 Pre-Waxed.
Tail	Brown Hackle Fibers.
Hackle	Brown Palmered over body.
Body	Peacock Herl.
Wing	Gray Squirrel Tail.
Head	Peacock Herl.

Hornberg

Hook	Mustad 9672 or equivalent.
Size	8 to 12
Thread	Black - 6/0 Pre-Waxed.
Body	Flat Silver Tinsel or Mylar.
Wing	2 Yellow Hackle Tips inside 2 Mallard Flank Feathers.
Cheek	Jungle Cock Eyes or Slip of Barred Wood Duck.
Hackle	Brown and Grizzly mixed.

Dark Cahill

Hook	Mustad 3906 or equivalent.
Size	10 to 14
Thread	Black - 6/0 Pre-Waxed.
Tail	Brown Hackle Fibers.
Body	Muskrat Fur Dubbing (muskrat).
Hackle	Brown Hen - Collar Style.
Wing	Lemon Wood Duck.

Light Cahill

Hook	Mustad 3906 or equivalent.
Size	10 to 14
Thread	Tan - 6/0 Pre-Waxed.
Tail	Dark Cream Hackle Fibers.
Body	Cream Dubbing (buff fox).
Hackle	Dark Cream Hen - Collar Style.
Wing	Lemon Wood Duck.

Dark Hendrickson

Hook	Mustad 3906 or equivalent.
Size	10 to 14
Thread	Gray - 6/0 Pre-Waxed.
Tail	Medium Dun Hackle Fibers.
Body	Muskrat Fur Dubbing (muskrat).
Hackle	Medium Dun Hen - Collar Style.
Wing	Lemon Wood Duck.

Quill Gordon

Hook	Mustad 3906 or equivalent.
Size	10 to 14
Thread	Gray - 6/0 Pre-Waxed.
Tail	Medium Dun Hackle Fibers.
Rib	Fine Gold Wire.
Body	Stripped Peacock Eye Quill.
Hackle	Medium Dun Hen - Collar Style.
Wing	Lemon Wood Duck.

Professor

Hook	Mustad 3906 or equivalent.
Size	10 to 14
Thread	Black - 6/0 Pre-Waxed.
Tail	Red Hackle Fibers.
Rib	Flat Gold Tinsel or Mylar.
Body	Yellow Fur or Floss.
Hackle	Brown Hen - Collar Style.
Wing	Gray Mallard Flank.

Pheasant Tail

Hook	Mustad 3906 or equivalent.
Size	10 to 16
Thread	Brown - 6/0 Pre-Waxed.
Tail	Mahogany Ringneck Pheasant Center Tail Fibers.
Rib	Fine Copper Wire.
Body	Mahogany Ringneck Pheasant Center Tail Fibers (same as Tail.
Hackle	Brown Partridge Hackle - Collar Style.

American March Brown

Hook	Mustad 3906 or equivalent.
Size	10 to 14
Thread	Black - 6/0 Pre-Waxed.
Tail	Dark Ginger Hackle Fibers.
Rib	Yellow Thread.
Body	Fawn Fox Fur (mink).
Hackle	Dark Ginger Hen - Collar Style.
Wing	Oak Turkey or Speckled Hen Wing Quill Segments.

Parmachene Belle

Hook	Mustad 3906 or equivalent.
Size	8 to 12
Thread	Black - 6/0 Pre-Waxed.
Tail	Red & White Hackle Fibers mixed.
Rib	Flat Gold Tinsel or Mylar.
Body	Yellow Fur or Floss.
Hackle	Red and White mixed - Collar Style.
Wing	Red and White Duck Quill Segments married.

Royal Coachman

Hook	Mustad 3906 or equivalent.
Size	8 to 14
Thread	Black - 6/0 Pre-waxed.
Tail	Golden Pheasant Tippet Fibers.
Body	Peacock Herl with Red Floss Center Band.
Hackle	Coachman Brown Hen - Collar Style.
Wing	White Duck Wing Quill Segments.

Black Gnat

Hook	Mustad 3906 or equivalent.
Size	10 to 14
Thread	Black - 6/0 Pre-Waxed.
Tail	Black Hackle Fibers.
Body	Black Fur Dubbing (black).
Hackle	Black Hen - Collar Style.
Wing	Mallard Wing Quill Segments.

Coachman

Hook	Mustad 3906 or equivalent.
Size	10 to 14
Thread	Black - 6/0 Pre-Waxed.
Tag	Flat Gold Tinsel or Mylar.
Body	Peacock Herl.
Hackle	Dark Ginger Hen - Collar Style.
Wing	White Duck Wing Quill Segments.

Leadwing Coachman

Hook	Mustad 3906 or equivalent.
Size	10 to 14
Thread	Black - 6/0 Pre-Waxed.
Tag	Flat Gold Tinsel or Mylar.
Body	Peacock Herl.
Hackle	Dark Ginger Hen - Collar Style.
Wing	Mallard Wing Quill Segments.

Alder

Hook	Mustad 3906 or equivalent.
Size	10 to 14
Thread	Black - 6/0 Pre-Waxed.
Tag	Flat Gold Tinsel or Mylar.
Body	Peacock Herl.
Hackle	Black Hen - Collar Style.
Wing	Oak Turkey or Speckled Hen Quill Segment.

G. R. Hare's Ear

Hook	Mustad 3906 or equivalent.
Size	8 to 16
Thread	Black - 6/0 Pre-Waxed.
Tail	Brown Hackle Fibers.
Rib	Flat Gold Tinsel or Mylar.
Body	English Hare's Ears and Mask Fur mixed (rabbit and fox).
Hackle	Brown Hen - Collar Style or Guard Hair Plucked out at Thorax area.
Wing	Mallard Wing Quill Segments.

Ginger Quill

Hook	Mustad 3906 or equivalent.
Size	10 to 16
Thread	Tan - 6/0 Pre-Waxed.
Tail	Dark Cream Hackle Fibers.
Rib	Fine Gold Wire.
Body	Stripped Peacock Eyed Quill.
Hackle	Dark Cream Hen - Collar Style.
Wing	Mallard Wing Quill Segments.

Blue Wing Olive

Hook	Mustad 3906 or equivalent.
Size	14 to 18
Thread	Olive - 6/0 Pre-Waxed.
Tail	Medium Dun Hackle Fibers.
Body	Medium Olive Fur (olive).
Hackle	Medium Dun Hen - Collar Style.
Wing	Mallard Wing Quill Segments.

Blue Quill

Hook	Mustad 3906 or equivalent.
Size	12 to 16
Thread	Gray - 6/0 Pre-Waxed.
Tail	Medium Dun Hackle Fibers.
Rib	Fine Gold Wire.
Body	Stripped Peacock Eye Quill.
Hackle	Medium Dun Hen - Collar Style.
Wing	Mallard Wing Quill Segments.

Pale Evening Dun

Hook	Mustad 3906 or equivalent.
Size	12 to 16
Thread	Gray 6/0 Pre-Waxed.
Tail	Light Dun Hackle Fibers.
Body	Pale Yellow Fur (primrose).
Hackle	Light Dun Hen - Collar Style.
Wing	Light Gray Mallard Wing Quill Segments.

Blue Dun

Hook	Mustad 3906 or equivalent.
Size	10 to 14
Thread	Black - 6/0 Pre-Waxed.
Tail	Medium Dun Hackle Fibers.
Body	Muskrat Fur (muskrat).
Hackle	Medium Dun Hen - Collar Style.
Wing	Mallard Wing Quill Segments.

Cowdung

Hook	Mustad 3906 or equivalent.
Size	10 to 14
Thread	Black - 6/0 Pre-Waxed.
Tag	Flat Gold Tinsel or Mylar.
Body	Olive Fur or Floss.
Hackle	Dark Ginger Hen - Collar Style.
Wing	White Duck Wing Quill Segments dyed Tan.

Montreal

Hook	Mustad 3906
Size	8 to 14
Thread	Black
Tail	Red Hackle Fibers.
Body	Claret Floss.
Rib	Flat Gold Tinsel.
Hackle	Claret Hen - Collar Style.
Wing	Oak Turkey or Speckled Hen Quill Segments.

Grizzly King

Hook	Mustad 3906
Size	8 to 14
Thread	Black
Tail	Red Hackle Fibers.
Body	Green Floss.
Rib	Flat Silver Tinsel.
Hackle	Grizzly Hen - Collar Style.
Wing	Mallard Flank.

Early Brown Stone

Hook	Mustad 3906
Size	10 to 14
Thread	Gray
Body	Stripped Rhode Island Red Hackle Quill.
Wing	2 Light Dun Hackle Points Tied Flat over Body.

Gray Hackle

Hook	Mustad 3906
Size	8 to 14
Thread	Black
Tail	Red Hackle Fibers.
Body	Peacock Herl.
Hackle	Grizzly Hen - Collar Style.

CHAPTER 2   NYMPHS

Opening Comments

Fur Bodies

Generic shades of fur blends and furs from specific animals have been specified. The colors in parentheses refer to Orvis Spectrablend Colors. Natural furs are recommended for all dubbed body nymphs with the exception of the Floating Nymphs where synthetic materials are also acceptable.

Wing Cases

Single

The most common style wing case. The majority of Orvis Nymphs use this technique. The wing case is initially tied in at the bend of the hook or at the midpoint of the hook shank then pulled forward and tyed in at the eye. (See photos associated with each pattern.)

Double

Used primarily for Stonefly Nymphs. See tying instructions on page 183.

Various

Several patterns such as the Zug Bug Dragon and Leadwing Coachman Nymphs require a feather cut to shape and tied in at the head. (See photos associated with each pattern.)

Legs

The photos on page 94 define the various styles of legs referred to in the pattern descriptions. These same definitions also apply to Wet Flies, Streamer Flies, Steelhead Flies, Salmon Flies and Saltwater Flies, but may be listed as hackles or throats rather than legs.

Beard Style . . .

Tie in the appropriate material, such as hackle fibers, under the hook toward the hook bend.

Divided Style . . .

Tie in the appropriate material, such as hen hackle fibers, on top of the hook at the head extending toward the hook bend, lying over the thorax. Divide the material by pulling the wing case through the middle of the material and tie off at head.

Collar Style . . .

Tie in the appropriate material, such as a hen hackle, by the tip, Wrap around the hook shank 2 times in the conventional dry fly style and tie off at head. The collar material may be wrapped before or after the wing case has been tied off at the head. See photos associated with the pattern description to determine whether the collar is wrapped before or after the wing case is tied off at head for each pattern.

To simplify your fishing, tie and fish the All Purpose Nymphs. Three basic shades in three sizes, weighted and unweighted, to represent the familiar silhouette suggestive of most nymphal forms. Given this form, plus the choice of light, medium and dark tone, plus 3 sizes, big, medium and small, a fly rodder can successfully suggest the many underwater species which are at all seasons to be found in every trout stream.

Fished at the right level (from just under the surface to right down on the bottom) some one or two of these nymph patterns will take trout at any season.

When tying weighted and unweighted nymphs, a different colored thread should be used to differentiate between the two versions.

Light

Hook	Mustad 38941 or equivalent.
Size	8, 12, 16
Thread	Black - 6/0 Pre-Waxed.
Tail	Lemon Wood Duck Fibers.
Rib	Brown Silk or Floss.
Abdomen	Cream Fox (buff fox).
Wing Case	Mahogany Ringneck Tail Segment.
Thorax	Cream Fox (same as abdomen).
Legs	Dark Cream Hen Hackle - Divided Style.

Medium

Hook	Mustad 38941 or equivalent.
Size	8, 12, 16
Thread	Black - 6/0 Pre-Waxed.
Tail	Mahogany Ringneck Tail Fibers.
Rib	Fine Gold Wire.
Abdomen	Grayish Brown (red fox).
Wing Case	White Tip Turkey Tail Segment.
Thorax	Grayish Brown (same as abdomen).
Legs	Brown Hen Hackle - Divided Style.

Dark

Hook	Mustad 38941 or equivalent.
Size	8, 12, 16
Thread	Black - 6/0 Pre-Waxed.
Tail	Mahogany Ringneck Tail Fibers.
Rib	Fine Gold Wire.
Abdomen	Dark Brown Fur (beaver brown).
Wing Case	White Tip Turkey Tail Segment.
Thorax	Dark Brown Fur (same as abdomen).
Legs	Black Hen Hackle - Divided Style.

Flashabou Nymph

Hook	Orvis 1524.
Size	10 to 18.
Thread	Black.
Tail	Ringneck Pheasant Tail Fibers.
Body	Pearlescent Flashabou.
Thorax	Black Angora Goat Teased Out.
Wing Case	Pearlescent Flashabou.

Peacock Matt's Fur

Hook	Orvis 1510.
Size	12 to 16.
Thread	Tan.
Tail	Wood Duck.
Body	Cream Angora Goat.
Rib	Gold Wire.
Thorax	Cream Angora Goat Teased Out.
Wing Case	Peacock Herl.

Pheasant Tail

Hook	Orvis 1524
Size	12 to 20.
Thread	Brown.
Tail	Ringneck Pheasant Tail Fibers.
Body	Ringneck Pheasant Tail Fibers.
Rib	Copper Wire.
Thorax	Peacock Herl.
Wing Case	Ringneck Pheasant Tail Fibers.
Legs	Ends of Wing Case Tied Back and Clipped.

Carrot Nymph

Hook	Orvis 1642.
Size	10 to 18.
Thread	Brown.
Tail	Speckled Hen Saddle Fibers.
Body	Rusty Orange Floss.
Back	Peacock Herl.
Rib	Gold Wire.
Thorax	Peacock Herl Palmered with Brown Hackle.
Wing Case	Pearlescent Flashabou.

Marabou Nymph

Hook   Mustad 3906B
Size   10 to 18
Thread   To Match Body Color.
Body   Marabou Dubbed on Thread.
Legs,⎤   Moose Body Hair Tied in at Bend
Back,⎬   of Hook with Fine Gold Wire
Wing ⎬   and Pulled Forward and Ribbed
Case⎦   with the Wire to Form the Back,
          Wing Case and Legs.
Note: Alternate patterns may be
          obtained by varying the body
          color.

Corixa Bug

Hook   Mustad 3906B
Size   12 to 16
Thread   Black.
Body   Silver Tinsel.
Back   Ringneck Center Tail Fibers.
Legs   Ringneck Center Tail Fibers.

Bitch Creek Nymph

Hook   Mustad 9672
Size   2 to 10
Thread   Black
Tail   White Living Rubber.
Body   Woven Black and Orange Chenille.
Hackle   Brown Palmered Over Front
          Half of Body.
Antennae White Living Rubber.

Helgramite

Hook   Orvis 1526.
Size   4 to 10.
Thread   Olive
Tail   Black Goose Biots.
Body   Brown/Olive Dubbing Teased Out.
Back   Brown Swiss Straw.
Rib   Gold Wire.
Thorax   Brown/Olive Dubbing Teased Out.
Wing Case Brown Swiss Straw.
Feelers   Black Goose Biots.

Breadcrust

Hook	Mustad 3906B or equivalent.
Size	8 to 14
Thread	Black - 6/0 Pre-Waxed.
Rib	Stripped Ruffed Grouse Tail Quill.
Body	Orange Wool or Fur.
Legs	Grizzly Hen Hackle - Collar Style.

Golden Quill

Hook	Mustad 3906B or equivalent.
Size	8 to 14
Thread	Yellow - 6/0 pre-Waxed.
Tail	2 Mallard Wing Quill Fibers from Leading Edge of Quill.
Rib 1	Fine Gold Wire.
Rib 2	Stripped Mallard Quill.
Body	Yellow Floss.
Legs	Partridge Hackle or equivalent - Collar Style.

Hendrickson Wiggle Nymph

Hook	Mustad 3906 or Equivalent.
Size	10 to 14
Thread	Olive
Tail	Wood Duck Flank Fiber.
Abdomen	1/3 Claret and 2/3 Natural Beaver.
Wing Case	Light Gray Goose Quill Segment.
Thorax	Same as Abdomen.
Legs	Brown Speckled Hen Fibers Divided Style.

Otter

Hook	Mustad 3906B or equivalent.
Size	10 to 16
Thread	Black - 6/0 Pre-Waxed.
Tail	Gray Mallard Flank Fibers.
Abdomen	Otter Fur.
Wing Case	Gray Mallard Flank.
Thorax	Otter Fur.
Legs	Gray Mallard Flank - Divided Style.

See Page 94 for tying instructions and page 194 for additional patterns.

Casual Dress

Hook	Mustad 9672
Size	6 to 12
Thread	Black
Tail	Muskrat Guard Hairs and Underfur.
Body	Rough Muskrat Dubbing.
Collar	Muskrat Guard Hairs and Underfur
Head	Black Ostrich Herl.
Note	Fly is Most Effective When Weighted.

Fledermouse

Hook	Mustad 9671 or 9672
Size	8 to 14
Thread	Brown
Body	Grayish Brown Australian Opossum.
Collar	Pine Squirrel Guard Hairs and Underfur.
Wing Case	Widgeon or Teal Dyed Dark Brown.

Jennings Nymph

Hook	Mustad 3906B
Size	8 to 14
Thread	Black
Tail	Ringneck Pheasant Tail.
Body	1/3 Claret and 2/3 Black African Goat Blended together.
Rib	Fine Oval Gold Tinsel.
Thorax	Peacock Herl
Collar	Speckled Hen Body Feather.

Red Squirrel Nymph

Hook	Orvis 1526.
Size	6 to 16.
Thread	Brown.
Tail	Hare's Mask Guard Hairs.
Body	Red Squirrel Belly Fur or Orvis Red Squirrel Substitute.
Rib	Fine Gold Oval Tinsel.

Leadwing Coachman

Hook   Mustad 9672 or equivalent.
Size   10 and 12
Thread   Black - 6/0 Pre-Waxed.
Tail   Brown Hackle Tip.
Body   Peacock Herl.
Hackle   Brown Hackle Fibers - Beard Style.
Wing Case Mallard Wing Shoulder Feather.

Black Quill

Hook   Mustad 3906B or equivalent.
Size   10 to 16
Thread   Black - 6/0 Pre-Waxed.
Tail   Medium Dun Hackle Fibers.
Abdomen   Stripped Peacock Eyed Quill.
Wing Case Mallard Wing Quill Segment.
Thorax   Muskrat Fur.
Legs   Medium Dun Hen - Divided Style.

Light Cahill

Hook   Mustad 3906B or equivalent.
Size   10 to 18
Thread   Cream - 6/0 Pre-Waxed.
Tail   Lemon Wood Duck Fibers.
Abdomen   Creamy Tan Fur (buff fox).
Wing Case Lemon Wood Duck.
Thorax   Creamy Tan Fur (buff fox).
Legs   Lemon Wood Duck - Divided Style.

Catskill March Brown

Hook   Mustad 9671 or equivalent.
Size   10
Thread   Orange - 6/0 Pre-Waxed.
Tail   Mahogany Ringneck Tail Fibers.
Rib   Brown Floss or Silk.
Abdomen   Amber Fur (amber).
Wing Case Ringneck Pheasant Short Tail
          Segments.
Thorax   Amber Fur (same as abdomen).
Legs   Brown Partridge Hackle - Collar
          Style.

Blue Wing Olive

Hook   Mustad 3906B or equivalent.
Size   14 to 18
Thread   Olive - 6/0 Pre-Waxed.
Tail   Lemon Wood Duck Fibers.
Rib   Brown Silk or Floss.
Abdomen Medium Olive Fur (olive).
Wing Case Goose Wing Quill Segment.
Thorax   Med. Olive Fur (same as abdomen).
Legs   Brown Partridge Hackle - Divided
          Style.

Catskill Canadensis

Hook   Mustad 9671 or equivalent.
Size   12
Thread   Orange - 6/0 Pre-Waxed.
Tail   Mahogany Ringneck Tail Fibers.
Rib   Brown Silk or Floss.
Abdomen Amber Fur (amber).
Wing Case Ringneck Short Tail Segment.
Thorax   Amber Fur (same as abdomen).
Legs   Brown Partridge Hackle - Collar
          Style.

Dark Hendrickson

Hook   Mustad 3906B or equivalent.
Size   10 to 14
Thread   Olive - 6/0 Pre-Waxed.
Tail   Lemon Wood Duck Fibers.
Rib   Brown Silk or Floss.
Abdomen Gray-Brown Fur (red fox).
Wing Case White Tip Turkey Tail Segment.
Thorax   Gray-Brown Fur (same as
          abdomen).
Legs   Brown Partridge Hackle - Divided
          Style.

Dun Variant

Hook   Mustad 9672 or equivalent.
Size   10
Thread   Olive - 6/0 Pre-Waxed.
Tail   Peacock Herl Tied Short.
Body   Claret and Black African Goat
          mixed.
Legs   Brown Partridge Hackle - Collar
          Style.

Quill Gordon

Hook	Mustad 3906B or equivalent.
Size	10 to 14
Thread	Olive - 6/0 Pre-Waxed.
Tail	Mahogany Ringneck Tail Fibers.
Rib	Brown Silk or Floss.
Abdomen	Beaver Belly (lt. beaver).
Wing Case	Brown Mottled Turkey Tail Segment.
Thorax	Beaver Belly (same as abdomen).
Legs	Brown Partridge Hackle - Divided Style.

Green Drake

Hook	Mustad 9672 or equivalent.
Size	10 to 12
Thread	Olive - 6/0 Pre-Waxed.
Tail	Mahogany Ringneck Tail Fibers.
Rib	Olive Silk or Floss.
Abdomen	Olive-Tan Fur (golden olive).
Wing Case	White Tip Turkey Tail Segment.
Thorax	Olive-Tan Fur (same as abdomen).
Legs	Lemon Wood Duck - Divided Style.

Catskill Hendrickson

Hook	Mustad 9671 or equivalent.
Size	10 to 12
Thread	Olive - 6/0 Pre-Waxed.
Tail	Lemon Wood Duck Fibers.
Rib	Fine Gold Wire.
Abdomen	Grayish-Brown Fur (pink fox).
Wing Case	Light Gray Goose or Duck Quill Segment.
Thorax	Grayish-Brown (same as abdomen).
Legs	Brown Partridge Hackle - Collar Style.

Mahogany

Hook	Mustad 3906B or equivalent.
Size	12 to 16
Thread	Olive - 6/0 Pre-Waxed.
Tail	Mahogany Ringneck Tail Fibers.
Rib	Tan Silk or Floss.
Abdomen	Reddish Gray Fur (claret).
Wing Case	Brown Mottled Turkey Tail Segment.
Thorax	Reddish Gray (same as abdomen).
Legs	Brown Partridge Hackle - Divided Style.

Atherton Medium

Hook   Mustad 3906B or equivalent.
Size   10 to 18
Thread   Black - 6/0 Pre-Waxed.
Tail   Mahogany Ringneck Tail Fibers.
Rib   Gold Oval Tinsel.
Abdomen   Hare's Ear and Mask Fur mixed
          (hare's ear).
Wing Case Goose Quill Segment Dyed King-
          fish Blue.
Thorax   (same as abdomen).
Legs   Brown Partridge Hackle - Divided
          Style.

American March Brown

Hook   Mustad 3906B or equivalent.
Size   10 to 14
Thread   Black - 6/0 Pre-Waxed.
Tail   Dark Moose Mane Fibers.
Rib   Stripped Peacock Eyed Quill.
Abdomen   Brown Floss.
Wing Case Mallard Wing Quill Segment.
Legs   Brown Hackle Palmered through
          Thorax.
Thorax   Peacock Herl.

Slate Wing Olive

Hook   Mustad 3906B or equivalent.
Size   14 to 20
Thread   Olive - 6/0 Pre-Waxed.
Tail   3 Canada Goose Quill Fibers.
Rib   Gray Silk or Floss.
Abdomen   Brownish Gray Fur (red fox).
Wing Case Canada Goose Quill Segment.
Thorax   Brownish Gray Fur (same as
          abdomen).
Legs   Medium Dun Hen - Divided Style.

Blue Quill

Hook   Mustad 3906B or equivalent.
Size   12 to 18
Thread   Black - 6/0 Pre-Waxed.
Tail   Mahogany Ringneck Tail Fibers.
Abdomen   Yellow Brown Fur (amber).
Wing Case Black Goose Quill Segment.
Thorax   Yellow Brown Fur (same as
          abdomen).
Legs   Ginger Hen - Divided Style.

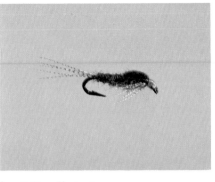

Olive Dun

Hook   Mustad 3906B or equivalent.
Size   12 to 18
Thread   Brown - 6/0 Pre-Waxed.
Tail   Mahogany Ringneck Tail Fibers.
Rib   Brown Silk or Floss.
Abdomen   Olive Gray Fur (gray olive).
Wing Case Light Canada Goose Quill Segment.
Thorax   Olive Gray Fur (same as abdomen).
Legs   Brown Hen Hackle - Divided Style.

Small Dun Variant

Hook   Mustad 3906B or equivalent.
Size   16 to 18
Thread   Brown - 6/0 Pre-Waxed.
Tail   Lemon Wood Duck Fibers.
Rib   Fine Copper Wire.
Abdomen   Dark Brown Fur (beaver brown).
Wing Case Dark Canada Goose Quill Segment.
Thorax   Dark Brown Fur (same as abdomen).
Legs   Lemon Wood Duck Fibers - Divided Style.

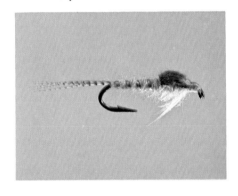

Pale Evening Dun

Hook   Mustad 3906B or equivalent.
Size   16 to 18
Thread   Olive - 6/0 Pre-Waxed.
Tail   Lemon Wood Duck Fibers.
Rib   Fine Gold Wire.
Abdomen   Grayish-Brown Fur (pink fox).
Wing Case Light Canada Goose Quill Segment.
Thorax   Grayish-Brown Fur (same as abdomen).
Legs   Brown Partridge Hackle - Divided Style.

Cream Variant

Hook   Mustad 9672 or equivalent.
Size   10 to 12
Thread   Tan - 6/0 Pre-Waxed.
Tail   Lemon Wood Duck Fibers.
Rib   Tan Silk or Floss.
Abdomen   Yellow-Tan Fur (amber).
Wing Case Light Canada Goose Quill Segment.
Thorax   Yellow-Tan Fur (same as abdomen).
Legs   Golden Ginger Hen Hackle - Divided Style.

Prince

Hook   Mustad 9671 or equivalent.
Size   8 to 12
Thread Black - 6/0 Pre-Waxed.
Weight Medium Lead Wire.
Tail   2 Red-Brown Goose Quill Fibers.
Rib   Flat Gold Tinsel or Mylar.
Body   Peacock Herl.
Legs   Brown Hackle Fibers - Collar Style.
Horns   2 White Goose Quill Fibers.

Tellico

Hook   Mustad 3906B or equivalent.
Size   10 to 14
Thread Black - 6/0 Pre-Waxed.
Weight Medium Lead Wire.
Tail   Guinea Hackle Fibers.
Wing Case Ringneck Short Tail Segment.
Rib   Peacock Herl.
Body   Yellow Floss.
Legs   Brown Hen - Collar Style.

Zug Bug

Hook   Mustad 3906B or equivalent.
Size   10 to 14
Thread Black - 6/0 Pre-Waxed.
Weight Medium Lead Wire.
Tail   Peacock Sword Fibers.
Rib   Flat Silver Tinsel or Mylar.
Body   Peacock Herl.
Legs   Brown Hen - Beard Style.
Wing Case Lemon Wood Duck tied in at head.

Beaver

Hook   Mustad 9671 or equivalent.
Size   10 to 12
Thread Gray - 6/0 Pre-Waxed.
Weight Medium Lead Wire.
Tail   Lemon Wood Duck.
Rib   Fine Gold Wire.
Body   Beaver Fur (lt. beaver).
Legs   Brown Partridge Hackle - Beard Style.

Olive Hare's Ear Nymph

Hook   Orvis 1642.
Size   8 to 18.
Thread   Olive.
Tail   Olive Hackle Fibers or Guard Hairs.
Body   Olive Hare's Mask Dubbing.
Rib   Fine Gold Mylar.
Thorax   Olive Hare's Mask Dubbing Teased Out.
Wing Case   Gray Goose Quill.

Peacock Creeper

Hook   Orvis 1524 - Inverted.
Size   8 to 14.
Thread   Red.
Tail   Peacock Sword Fibers.
Body   Peacock Herl.
Rib   Clear Body Glass or "V" Rib.
Wing Case   Hen Pheasant Body Feathers.
Legs   White Goose Biots.

Hare's Ear Creeper

Hook   Orvis 1524 Tied Inverted.
Size   8 to 14.
Thread   Brown.
Tail   Hare's Mask Guard Hairs.
Body   Hare's Mask Dubbing.
Rib   Clear Body Glass or "V" Rib.
Wing Cases Hen Ringneck Body Feather.
Legs   White Goose Biots Tied Forward.

G. R. Hare's Ear

Hook   Mustad 3906B or equivalent.
Size   8 to 16
Thread   Brown - 6/0 Pre-Waxed.
Weight   Medium Lead Wire.
Tail   Hare's Ear - Guard Hairs
Rib   Flat Gold Tinsel or Mylar.
Abdomen   Hare's Ear Fur (hare's ear).
Wing Case   Oak Turkey Wing Quill Segment.
Thorax   Hare's Ear Fur (same as abdomen).
Legs   Dubbing picked out in Thorax area.

Mosquito Larva

Hook	Orvis Supreme or equivalent.
Size	14 to 18
Thread	Black - 6/0 Pre-Waxed.
Tail	Grizzly Hackle Fibers.
Abdomen	Stripped Peacock Eyed Quill.
Thorax	Peacock Herl.
Feelers	Grizzly Hackle Fibers.

Brown Bomber

Hook	Mustad 3906B or equivalent.
Size	8 to 14
Thread	Black - 6/0 Pre-Waxed.
Rib	Flat Gold Tinsel or Mylar.
Body	Beaver Fur.
Legs	Partridge tied Collar Style.

Gray

Hook	Mustad 9671 or equivalent.
Size	8 to 12
Thread	Black - 6/0 Pre-Waxed.
Weight	Medium Lead Wire.
Tail	Grizzly Hackle Fibers.
Body	Muskrat (muskrat).
Legs	Grizzly Hen - Collar Style.

Dark Gray Larva

Hook	Mustad 38941 or Mustad 37160.
Size	12 to 16
Thread	Brown - 6/0 Pre-Waxed.
Rib	Fine Gold Wire.
Body	Hare's Ear and Mask Blend (hare's ear).
Legs	Brown Partridge Hackle - Beard Style.
Head	Dark Brown Fur (beaver brown).

White Larva

Hook	Mustad 38941 or Mustad 37160.
Size	10 to 16
Thread	Brown - 6/0 Pre-Waxed.
Rib	Fine Gold Wire.
Body	Dirty White Fur (white).
Legs	Brown Partridge Hackle - Beard Style.
Head	Dark Brown Fur (beaver brown).

Pale Olive Larva

Hook	Mustad 38941 or Mustad 37160.
Size	12 to 16
Thread	Brown - 6/0 Pre-Waxed.
Rib	Fine Gold Wire.
Body	Pale Olive Fur (pale olive).
Legs	Brown Partridge Hackle - Beard Style.
Head	Dark Brown Fur (beaver brown).

Yellow Larva

Hook	Mustad 38941 or Mustad 37160.
Size	12 to 16.
Thread	Brown - 6/0 Pre-Waxed.
Rib	Fine Gold Wire.
Body	Pale Yellow Fur (sulphur).
Legs	Brown Partridge Hackle - Beard Style.
Head	Dark Brown Fur (beaver brown).

Small Black Pupa

Hook   Orvis Premium or Mustad 37160
Size   16 to 20
Thread Brown - 6/0 Pre-Waxed.
Body   Blackish Brown Fur (iron blue dun).
Legs   Black Hen Hackle - Beard Style.
Head   Blackish Brown Fur (same as body).

Small Green Pupa

Hook   Orvis Premium or Mustad 37160.
Size   16 to 20
Thread Olive - 6/0 Pre-Waxed.
Body   Bright Olive Green Fur (olive green)
Legs   Brown Partridge Hackle - Beard Style.
Head   Bright Olive Green Fur (same as body).

Little Sand Sedge

Hook   Mustad 3906 or Mustad 37160.
Size   14 to 18
Thread Brown - 6/0 Pre-Waxed.
Body   Pale Yellow Fur (primrose).
Wing Case Mallard Quill Segments tied short at each side of body.
Legs   Brown Partridge Hackle - Beard Style.
Head   Medium Brown Fur (red fox).

Speckled Sedge

Hook   Mustad 3906 or Mustad 37160.
Size   12 to 16
Thread Brown - 6/0 Pre-Waxed.
Rib   Reddish Brown Fur (Australian Opossum).
Body   Light Brown Fur (mink).
Wing Case Mallard Quill Segments tied short on each side of body.
Legs   Brown Partridge Hackle - Divided Style.
Head   Dark Brown Fur (beaver brown).

Small Dark Pupa

Hook   Orvis Premium or Mustad 37160.
Size   16 to 22
Thread Brown - 6/0 Pre-Waxed.
Body   Hare's Ear Fur (hare's ear).
Legs   Brown Partridge Hackle - Beard
        Style
Head   Hare's Ear Fur (same as body).

Grannom Pupa

Hook   Mustad 3906 or Mustad 37160.
Size   12 to 16
Thread Brown - 6/0 Pre-Waxed.
Rib   Fine Gold Wire.
Body   Reddish Brown Fur (Australian
        Opossum).
Wing Case Mallard Quill Segments tied short
        on each side of body.
Legs   Brown Partridge Hackle - Beard
        Style.
Head   Dark Brown Fur (beaver brown).

Olive Sedge

Hook   Mustad 3906 or Mustad 37160.
Size   14 to 18
Thread Brown - 6/0 Pre-Waxed.
Body   Pale Olive Fur (pale olive).
Wing Case Mallard Quill Segments tied short
        on each side of body.
Legs   Brown Partridge Hackle - Beard
        Style.
Head   Dark Brown Fur (beaver brown).

Great Brown Sedge

Hook   Mustad 3906 or Mustad 37160.
Size   8 to 12
Thread Brown - 6/0 Pre-Waxed.
Rib   Fine Gold Wire.
Body   Dark Brown Fur (beaver brown).
Wing Case Mallard Quill Segments tied short
        on each side of body.
Legs   Brown Partridge Hackle - Beard
        Style.
Head   Blackish Brown Fur (iron blue dun)

Green Latex Pupa

Hook	Mustad 37160.
Size	12 to 22
Thread	Tan - 6/0 Pre-Waxed.
Under-	
Body	Heavy Cream Latex.
Over-	
Body	Thin Green Latex.
Wing Case	Mallard Quill Segments tied short on each side of body.
Legs	Red or Gray Squirrel Guard Hairs or Brown Partridge Hackle.
Head	Dark Brown Fur (beaver brown).

Cream Latex Pupa

Hook	Mustad 37160.
Size	12 to 22
Thread	Tan - 6/0 Pre-Waxed.
Under-	
Body	Heavy Cream Latex.
Over-	
Body	Thin Cream Latex.
Wing Case	Mallard Quill Segments tied short on each side of body.
Legs	Red or Gray Squirrel Guard Hairs or Brown Partridge Hackle.
Head	Dark Brown Fur (beaver brown).

Yellow Latex Larva

Hook	Mustad 37160.
Size	12 to 22
Thread	Tan - 6/0 Pre-Waxed.
Under-	
Body	Heavy Cream Latex.
Over-	
Body	Thin Yellow Latex.
Head	Dark Brown Fur (beaver brown).

Medium Case Caddis

Hook	Mustad 79580.
Size	8 to 14
Thread	Black - 6/0 Pre-Waxed.
Under-	
Body	Silver Tinsel Chenille.
Over-	
Body	Muskrat Fur.
Head	Black Ostrich Herl.

Diving Caddis

Hook   Mustad 94840
Size   12 to 18
Thread   Black
Body   Sparsely Dubbed Ultratranslucent
            Dubbing.
Underwing   Partridge Hackle Fibers.
Overwing   White Ultratranslucent Dubbing.
Hackle   Sparse Brown
Note: Body and hackle color may be
            varied to duplicate species in
            your area. Tan, Olive and Gray
            are the most popular.

Deep Sparkle Pupa

Hook   Mustad 94840
Size   12 to 20
Thread   Black
Body   Dubbed Underbody with Ultra-
            translucent Dubbing Tied in at
            Bend of Hook and Pulled Forward
            Over the Underbody.
Legs   Partridge Hackle.
Head   Dark Brown Dubbing.
Note: Body color may be varied to suit
            your needs.

Caddis Larva

Hook   Yorkshire Sedge Hook.
Size   12 to 16
Thread   Black
Body   Olive, White, Brown, Gray or
            Yellow Ultratranslucent
            Dubbing.
Legs   Brown Hackle Fibers.

Floating Pupa

Hook   Mustad 9672 - Bent to Shape.
Size   12 to 18
Thread   Black
Body   Sparsely Spun Deer Hair.
Head   Fluorescent Lime Ostrich.

Olive Tarcher

Hook	Mustad 37160
Size	16 to 20
Thread	Olive
Tail	Cock Ringneck Tail Fibers.
Abdomen	Olive Transluscent Dubbing.
Rib	Fine Oval Gold Tinsel
Wing	
Case	Speckled Hen Quill Segment.
Thorax	Same as Abdomen.
Legs	Brown Speckled Hen Fibers - Divided Style or Tied in with Wing Case and Pulled Over Thorax.
Note	See Page 194 for additional patterns.

Fur Caddis Pupa (Grannom)

Hook	Mustad 37160 or Partridge Sedge Hook.
Size	12 to 20
Thread	Brown
Body	Reddish Brown Australian Opossum.
Pupal	
Wings	Speckled Hen Quill Segments.
Legs &	
Head	Pine Squirrel Guard Hairs and Underfur.
Note	See Page 194 and 181 for additional patterns and tying instructions respectively.

Pale Green Transluscent Caddis Pupa

Hook	Mustad 37160 or 3906B
Size	10 to 18
Thread	Brown
Body	Pale Green Transluscent Dubbing.
Pupal	
Wing	Gray Swiss Straw.
Legs	Deer Body Hair.
Head	Dark Brown Transluscent Dubbing.
Antennae	Mallard Flank Fibers.
Note	See Page 194 for additional patterns.

Caddis Pupa

Hook	Mustad 37160 or Partridge Sedge
Size	10 to 18
Thread	Brown
Under	Green Mylar Tinsel.
Body	
Over	Clear Swannundaze.
Body	
Head &	Red Squirrel Guard Hairs and
Legs	Underfur Tied in the Same Manner as Described on the Opposite Page.

Note: Alternate colors also work well - Caddis Green and Transparent Black are especially good.

Birds Stonefly

Hook	Orvis 1526.
Size	6 to 12.
Thread	Orange.
Tail	Gray Goose Biots.
Body	Dark Brown Dubbing.
Rib	Orange Floss.
Thorax	Peacock Herl Palmered with Furnace Hackle.
Wing Case	Mottled Turkey Tail.

Stonefly Creeper

Hook	Mustad 9672 or equivalent.
Size	6 to 12
Thread	Yellow - 6/0 Pre-Waxed.
Tail	Mahogany Ringneck Pheasant Center Tail Fibers.
Wing Case	Barred Wood Duck Flank Feather.
Abdomen	Stripped Ginger Hackle Quill.
Thorax	Amber African Goat or equivalent.
Legs	Brown Partridge - Collar Style.

Black Swimming Stone

Hook	Orvis 1512.
Size	6 to 14.
Thread	Black.
Tail	Black Goose Biots.
Body	Black Antron® Dubbing.
Rib	Black Body Glass or "V" Rib.
Legs	Black Goose Biots.
Thorax	Black Antron® Dubbing.
Wing Case	Mottled Turkey Tail.
Note:	Amber is also an effective color.

Rubber Leg Stone

Hook	Orvis 1640.
Size	4 to 10.
Thread	Gray.
Tail	White Rubber Legs.
Body	Dark Brown and Golden Yellow Wool Woven with Yellow on Underside.
Legs	White Rubber Legs.
Thorax	Dark Gray Fur Dubbing with Guard Hairs Teased Out.

Swannundaze Stonefly (Style I)

Hook	Mustad 9672 or Partridge Strong-hold.
Size	4 to 12
Thread	Brown
Tail	Ringneck Pheasant Tail Fibers or Goose Quill Fibers.
Abdomen	Dk. Transparent Amber Swannundaze.
Rib	Natural Ostrich Herl.
Wing Cases	Speckled Hen Body Feather.
Thorax	Amber Transluscent Dubbing.
Legs	Speckled Hen Fibers.
Note	See Page 184 for Tying Instructions.

Swannundaze Stonefly (Style II)

Hook	Mustad 9672 or Partridge Stronghold
Size	4 to 12
Thread	Brown
Tail	Ringneck Pheasant Tail Fibers or Goose Quill Fibers.
Abdomen	Amber Transluscent Dubbing.
Rib	Dark Transparent Amber Swannundaze.
Wing Cases	Speckled Hen Body Feathers.
Thorax	Same as Abdomen.
Legs	Speckled Hen Fibers.

Ted's Stone Fly

Hook	Mustad 9672 or equivalent.
Size	6 to 12
Thread	Black - 6/0 Pre-Waxed.
Weight	Medium Lead Wire.
Tail	2 Red Brown Goose Quill Fibers.
Abdomen	Brown Chenille.
Wing Case	Brown Chenille.
Legs	Black Hackle Palmered through Thorax.
Thorax	Orange Chenille.

Montana

Hook	Mustad 9672 or equivalent.
Size	6 to 14
Thread	Black - 6/0 Pre-Waxed.
Weight	Medium Lead Wire.
Tail	Black Hackle Fibers.
Abdomen	Black Chenille.
Wing Case	Black Chenille.
Legs	Black Hackle Palmered through Thorax.
Thorax	Yellow Chenille.

Kaufmann's Brown Stone

Hook	Mustad 9575 or 3665A.
Size	2 to 10
Thread	Brown
Tail	Reddish Brown Goose Biots.
Body	Brown Ultratranslucent Dubbing.
Rib	Transparent Brown Swannundaze.
Wing Cases	Turkey Cut or Burned to Shape.
Antennae	Reddish Brown Goose Biots.

Dave's Stone Fly

Hook	Mustad 36890
Size	4 to 8
Thread	Black
Tail	Black Nylon.
Abdomen	Black Ultratranslucent Dubbing.
Back & Wing Cases	Black Swiss Straw.
Rib	Copper Wire.
Thorax	Rust Ultratranslucent Dubbing.
Legs	Hen Saddle.
Antennae	Black Nylon.

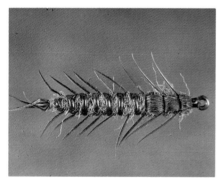

Helgrammite

Hook	Mustad 3665A
Size	2 to 10
Thread	Black
Tail	Black Goose Biots.
Abdomen	Black Ultratranslucent Dubbing.
Rib	Transparent Black Swannundaze.
Legs	Black Goose Biots.
Wing Case	White Tip Turkey Tail.
Thorax	Black Ultratranslucent Dubbing.

Shedding Stone Fly

Hook	Mustad 9672
Size	4 to 10
Thread	White
Tail	White Goose Biots.
Abdomen	White Latex.
Legs	White Goose Biots.
Wing Cases	Light Mottled Turkey.
Thorax	White Ultratranslucent Dubbing.

Early Black

Hook	Mustad 9671 or equivalent.
Size	10 to 14
Thread	Black - 6/0 Pre-Waxed.
Tail	2 Canada Goose Quill Fibers.
Abdomen	Dark Brownish Black Fur (iron blue dun).
Wing Case	Doubled Black Goose Quill Segment.
Thorax	Amber Fur (same as abdomen).
Legs	Dark Blue Dun Hen - Divided Style.

Early Brown

Hook	Mustad 9671 or equivalent.
Size	10 to 14
Thread	Tan - 6/0 Pre-Waxed.
Tail	2 White Tip Turkey Tail Fibers.
Abdomen	Medium Brown Fur (red fox).
Wing Case	Doubled White Tip Turkey Tail Segment.
Thorax	Med. Brown Fur (same as abdomen).
Legs	Brown Hen - Divided Style.

Little Yellow

Hook	Mustad 9671 or equivalent.
Size	12 to 16
Thread	Yellow - 6/0 Pre-Waxed.
Tail	2 Amber Goose Quill Fibers.
Abdomen	Amber Fur (amber).
Wing Case	Doubled Cinnamon Turkey Quill Segments.
Thorax	Amber Fur (same as abdomen).
Legs	Pale Yellow Hen - Divided Style.

Perla

Hook	Mustad 38941 slightly bent.
Size	6 to 10
Thread	Tan - 6/0 Pre-Waxed.
Tail	2 Amber Goose Quill Fibers.
Abdomen	Amber Blend (amber and yellow African Goat).
Wing Case	Double Mottled Turkey Quill Segment.
Thorax	Amber Blend (same as abdomen).
Legs	Tan Ringneck Body Feather - Divided Style.

Giant Black

Hook	Mustad 38941 slightly bent.
Size	4 to 8
Thread	Black - 6/0 Pre-Waxed.
Tail	2 Dark Canada Goose Quill Fibers.
Abdomen	Brownish Black Fur (iron blue dun and brown African Goat).
Wing Case	Doubled White Tip Turkey Tail Segment.
Thorax	Brownish Black Fur (same as abdomen).
Legs	Natural Black Hen - Divided Style.

Giant Golden

Hook	Mustad 38941 slightly bent.
Size	4 to 8
Thread	Tan - 6/0 Pre-Waxed.
Tail	2 Amber Goose Quill Fibers.
Rib	Medium Brown Fur (red fox).
Abdomen	Tan Fox (sandy fox).
Wing Case	Doubled Mottled Turkey Quill Segment.
Thorax	Tan Fox (same as abdomen).
Legs	Tan Ringneck Body Feather - Divided Style.

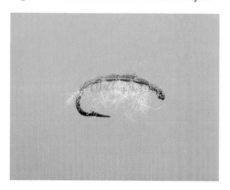

Olive Scud

Hook	Mustad 3906B or equivalent.
Size	10 to 16
Thread	Olive - 6/0 Pre-Waxed.
Tail	Pale Olive Fur (pale olive).
Rib	Fine Gold Wire.
Wing Case	Mallard Quill Segment.
Body	Pale Olive Fur (pale olive).
Legs	Picked out Body Fur.

Sow Bug

Hook	Mustad 3906B or equivalent.
Size	10 to 16
Thread	Gray - 6/0 Pre-Waxed.
Tail	2 Mallard Quill Fibers.
Rib	Fine Silver Wire.
Wing Case	Polyethylene Strip.
Body	Muskrat.
Legs	Picked out Body Fur.

Parachute Damsel

Hook	Orvis 1638.
Size	8 to 12.
Thread	Black.
Body	Bright Blue Deer Body Hair Tied Extended.
Wing Case/	
Head	Bright Blue Deer Body Hair.
Hackle	Light Dun Wound Around Base of Wing Case.

Floating Dragon Nymph

Hook	Orvis 1526.
Size	8 to 12.
Thread	Brown.
Tail	Brown Marabou.
Body	Spun Brown Deer Body Hair Clipped to Shape.
Wing Case	Mottled Turkey Tail.
Legs	Ringneck Center Tail Fibers.
Head	Brown Dubbing.
Eyes	Burned Back Monofilament.

Damsel Nymph

Hook	Orvis 1523.
Size	10 to 14.
Thread	Olive.
Tail	Yellow dyed Grizzly Hackle tips tied long.
Body	Olive Ostrich Hen tied over tail butts and on to hook shank.
Wing Cases	Dyed Brown Turkey Quill.
Eyes	Burned Back Monofilament.

Dragon Nymph

Hook	Orvis 1526.
Size	8 to 12.
Thread	Brown.
Tail	Brown Marabou.
Body	Brown Dubbing.
Rib	Copper Wire.
Wing Case	Mottled Turkey Tail.
Legs	Ringneck Pheasant Tail Fibers.
Head	Brown Dubbing.
Eyes	Burned Back Monofilament.
Note:	May also be tied in Dark Olive.

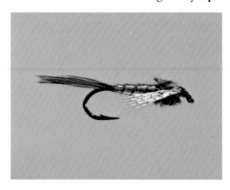

Dragon

Hook	Mustad 9671 or equivalent.
Size	6 to 10
Thread	Black - 6/0 Pre-Waxed.
Body	Olive Chenille.
Wing	Mallard Wing Shoulder Feather.
Legs	Black Hen Hackle - Collar Style.

Damsel

Hook	Mustad 9672 or equivalent.
Size	8 to 12
Thread	Black - 6/0 Pre-Waxed.
Tail	2 Brown Hackle Tips.
Rib	Single Strand Brown Floss or Cotton.
Abdomen	Light Olive Floss.
Wing Case	White Tip Turkey Tail Segment.
Thorax	Olive Chenille.
Legs	Gray Mallard Flank Fibers.

Damsel Fly Nymph

Hook	Mustad 9672 or Partridge Stronghold
Size	6 to 10
Thread	Olive
Tail	Olive Maribou
Abdomen	Dark Transparent Olive Swannundaze.
Rib	Olive Ostrich Herl
Wing Case	Gray Partridge Dyed Olive.
Thorax	Olive Transluscent Dubbing.
Legs	Gray Partridge Dyed Olive.

Assam Dragon

Hook	Mustad 9679
Size	6 to 10
Thread	Brown, Olive or Black
Body	Mole Fur Dyed Brown, Olive or Black. Cut a Strip of Mole Hide 1/16 inch Wide. Taper at End, Tie in and Wrap Toward Eye.
Collar	Speckled Hen Body Feather.
Eye	Bead Chain Painted to Match Body.

Pancora Crab

Hook	Orvis 1645.
Size	2 to 6.
Thread	Red.
Body	Olive Rabbit fur Strip Wound around Hook Shank.
Hackle	Ringneck Pheasant Rump Feather.

Pancora Wooly Worm

Hook	Orvis 1511.
Size	2 to 6.
Thread	Black.
Tail	Orange Marabou.
Body	Olive Chenille Palmered with Olive Grizzly Hackle.

Lord's Killer

Hook	Orvis 1642.
Size	6 to 10.
Thread	Black.
Tail	Moose Body Hair.
Body	Orange Chenille.
Wing	Chuckar Partridge tied in on each side of Hook.

Mrs. Simpson

Hook	Orvis 1642.
Size	6 to 10.
Thread	Black.
Tail	Black Squirrel Tail under Cock Ringneck Pheasant Body Feather.
Body	Red Wool.
Wing	Cock Ringneck Pheasant Body Feathers Tied in on each side of hook.

Greenwell's Glory

Hook	Partridge L3B or Mustad 94842.
Size	12 to 18
Thread	Olive
Wing	Mallard Quill Segments (Blackbird).
Tail	Greenwell Fibers (Furnace).
Body	Olive Dubbing.
Rib	Fine Gold Wire.
Hackle	Coch-y-Bondu

Mill Evening Dun

Hook	Partridge L3B or Mustad 94842.
Size	12 to 18
Thread	Black
Wing	Mallard Quill Segments (Coot).
Tail	Grizzly Hackle Fibers.
Body	Flat Gold Tinsel.
Hackle	Light Grizzly.

Kite's Imperial

Hook	Partridge L3B or Mustad 94842.
Size	12 to 18
Thread	Black
Tail	Ginger Hackle Fibers (Honey).
Body	Gray Goose (Heron) Wing Quill Fibers Wound as a Body.
Rib	Fine Gold Tinsel.
Hackle	Ginger (Honey).

Lunn's Particular

Hook	Partridge L3B or Mustad 94842.
Size	12 to 18
Thread	Red
Wing	Blue Dun Hackle Tips Tied Spent.
Tail	Brown Hackle Fibers.
Body	Sherry Floss.
Rib	Stripped Ginger Hackle Quill.
Hackle	Brown.

Invicta

Hook	Partridge A or Mustad 3906.
Size	10 to 16
Thread	Black
Tail	Golden Pheasant Crest.
Body	Dirty Yellow Dubbing.
Rib	Palmered Brown Hackle with Oval Gold Tinsel.
Throat	Guinea Hackle Dyed Blue (Blue Jay).
Wing	Hen Ringneck Pheasant Center Tail Segment.

Mallard and Claret

Hook	Partridge A or Mustad 3906.
Size	10 to 16
Thread	Black
Tail	Golden Pheasant Tippet.
Body	Claret Seal or Angora Goat.
Rib	Fine Oval Gold Tinsel.
Throat	Brown Hen Hackle (or Claret).
Wing	Bronze Mallard.

Red Palmer

Hook	Partridge A or Mustad 3906.
Size	10 to 16
Thread	Red
Body	Sherry Seal.
Rib	Palmered Brown Hackle with Oval Gold Tinsel.
Hackle	Brown.

Black and Peacock Spider

Hook	Partridge A or Mustad 3906.
Size	10 to 16
Thread	Black
Body	Peacock Herl Tied Full.
Rib	Fine Gold Wire
Hackle	Black Hen Hackle.

Demoiselle

Hook	Partridge H1A or Mustad 9671.
Size	10 to 14 Weighted
Thread	Brown
Tail	Green Hackle Fibers.
Body	Green Highlander Seal Blended with a Small Amount of Red Seal.
Rib	Fine Flat Gold Tinsel.
Hackle	Partridge Dyed Golden Olive.

Shrimper

Hook	Partridge A or Mustad 3906.
Size	10 to 14 Weighted
Thread	Brown
Body	Pale Olive Seal Fur with Polyethylene Pulled Over Back.
Rib	Palmered Olive Hackle with Orange Floss.

Black Hatching Midge Pupa

Hook	Partridge A or Mustad 3906.
Size	10 to 16
Thread	Black
Tail	White Floss.
Abdomen	Black Floss Ribbed with Fine Flat Silver Tinsel Then a Polyethylene Strip is Wound Over The Floss and Rib.
Thorax	Peacock Herl.
Breathing Filaments	White Polypropylene Yarn.

Bloodworm Larva

Hook	Partridge H1A or Mustad 9671.
Size	8 to 14
Thread	Black
Tail	Red Marabou
Body	Red Floss with Three Evenly Spaced Bulges
Head	Peacock Herl.

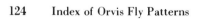

Black Nose Dace

Hook   Mustad 9575 or Mustad 3665A.
Size   6 to 12
Thread   Black - 6/0 Pre-Waxed.
Tag   Red Monocord to secure end of Mylar Piping Body.
Body   Fine Silver Mylar Piping.
Wing   Brown Bucktail over Black Dyed Squirrel Tail over White Bucktail sparsely tied.

Mickey Finn

Hook   Mustad 9575 or Mustad 3665A.
Size   6 to 12
Thread   Black - 6/0 Pre-Waxed.
Tag   Red Monocord to secure end of Mylar Piping Body.
Body   Fine Silver Mylar Piping.
Wing   Yellow Bucktail over Red Bucktail over Yellow Bucktail sparsely tied.

Silver Darter

Hook   Mustad 9575 or Mustad 3665A.
Size   4 to 10
Thread   Black - 6/0 Pre-Waxed.
Tag   Red Monocord to secure end of Mylar Piping.
Body   Fine Silver Mylar Piping.
Throat   Peacock Sword Fibers.
Wing   4 Badger Saddle Hackles.

Golden Darter

Hook   Mustad 9575 or Mustad 3665A.
Size   4 to 10
Thread   Black - 6/0 Pre-Waxed.
Tag   Red Monocord to secure end of Mylar Piping.
Body   Fine Gold Mylar Piping.
Throat   Jungle Cock Hackle Tip or Guinea Hackle Fibers.
Wing   4 Furnace Saddle Hackles.

Gray Ghost

Hook   Mustad 9575 or Mustad 3665A.
Size   2 to 12
Thread   Black - 6/0 Pre-Waxed.
Tag   Flat Silver Tinsel or Mylar.
Body   Orange Floss.
Rib   Flat Silver Tinsel or Mylar.
Throat   3 or 4 strands of Peacock Herl over
           sparse bunch of White Bucktail over
           Golden Pheasant Crest curving upward.
Wing   4 Gray Saddle Hackles over Golden
           Pheasant Crest curving downward.
Shoulders Silver Pheasant Body Feathers. — Cheek Jungle Cock.

Grizzly King

Hook   Mustad 9575 or Mustad 3665A.
Size   6 to 12
Thread   Black - 6/0 Pre-Waxed.
Tail   Red Hackle Fibers.
Rib   Flat Silver Tinsel.
Body   Green Floss.
Throat   Grizzly Hackle Fibers.
Wing   4 Grizzly Saddle Hackles.

Royal Coachman Bucktail

Hook   Mustad 9575 or Mustad 3665A.
Size   4 to 12
Thread   Black - 6/0 Pre-Waxed.
Tail   Golden Pheasant Tippet Fibers.
Body   Peacock Herl with a Red Floss
           Center Band.
Throat   Brown Hackle Fibers.
Wing   White Bucktail.

Light Spruce

Hook   Mustad 79580.
Size   2 to 10
Thread   Black - 6/0 Pre-Waxed.
Tail   Peacock Sword Fibers.
Body   1/2 Red Floss, 1/2 Peacock Herl.
Wing   4 Badger Saddle Hackles.
Throat   Badger Hackle - Collar Style.

Red Matuka

Hook	Mustad 9672 or Mustad 38941.
Size	2 to 10
Thread	Black - 6/0 Pre-Waxed.
Rib	Fine Oval Gold Tinsel.
Body	Red Aunt Lydia's Rug Yarn.
Wing	4 Badger Hen Hackles.
Hackle	Badger Hen.

Gray Matuka

Hook	Mustad 9672 or Mustad 38941.
Size	2 to 10
Thread	Black - 6/0 Pre-Waxed.
Rib	Fine Oval Silver Tinsel.
Body	Steel Gray Aunt Lydia's Rug Yarn.
Wing	4 Grizzly Hen Hackles.
Hackle	Grizzly Hen.

Olive Matuka

Hook	Mustad 9672 or Mustad 38941.
Size	2 to 10
Thread	Olive - 6/0 Pre-Waxed.
Rib	Fine Oval Gold Tinsel.
Body	Light Avocado Aunt Lydia's Rug Yarn.
Wing	4 Olive Hen Hackles.
Hackle	Olive Hen.

Yellow Matuka

Hook	Mustad 9672 or Mustad 38941.
Size	2 to 10
Thread	Tan - 6/0 Pre-Waxed.
Rib	Fine Gold Oval Tinsel.
Body	Yellow Aunt Lydia's Rug Yarn.
Wing	4 Furnace Hen Hackles.
Hackle	Furnace Hen.

See Page 185 for Tying Instructions.

Black Nose Dace

Hook	Mustad 36620 or equivalent.
Size	2 to 10
Thread	Red - 6/0 Pre-Waxed.
Body	Flat Silver Tinsel or Mylar.
Lateral	
Stripe	Black Bucktail or dyed Squirrel Tail.
Back	Brown Bucktail.
Belly	White Bucktail.
Eye	Lacquered Yellow with Black Dot.

Silver Shiner

Hook	Mustad 36620 or equivalent.
Size	2 to 10
Thread	Red - 6/0 Pre-Waxed.
Body	Flat Silver Tinsel or Mylar.
Back	Brown Bucktail.
Belly	White Bucktail.
Eye	Lacquered Yellow with Black Dot.

Red Fin Shiner

Hook	Mustad 36620 or equivalent.
Size	2 to 10
Thread	Red - 6/0 Pre-Waxed.
Rib	Flat Silver Tinsel or Mylar.
Body	Red Floss.
Back	Brown Bucktail.
Belly	White Bucktail.
Eye	Lacquered Yellow with Black Dot.

Golden Shiner

Hook	Mustad 36620 or equivalent.
Size	2 to 10
Thread	Red - 6/0 Pre-Waxed.
Body	Flat Gold Tinsel or Mylar.
Lateral	
Stripe	Yellow Bucktail.
Back	Brown Bucktail.
Belly	White Bucktail.
Eye	Lacquered Yellow with Black Dot.

See Page 187 for Tying Instructions.

Llama

Hook	Mustad 38941.
Size	4 to 10
Thread	Black - 6/0 Pre-Waxed.
Rib	Flat Gold Tinsel or Mylar.
Body	Red Floss.
Wing	Woodchuck Hair.
Hackle	Grizzly Hen - Collar Style.
Eyes	Lacquered White with Black Dot.

Muddler Minnow

Hook	Mustad 38941.
Size	2 to 12
Thread	Black - Pre-Waxed Monocord.
Tail	Mottled Turkey Quill Segment.
Body	Flat Gold Tinsel or Mylar.
Under-	
Wing	Gray Squirrel Tail.
Overwing	Mottled Turkey Quill Segments.
Head	Spun Natural Gray Deer Hair, clipped to shape leaving several strands extending toward bend.

Yellow Muddler Minnow

Hook	Mustad 38941.
Size	2 to 12
Thread	Black - Pre-Waxed Monocord.
Tail	Yellow Turkey Quill Segment.
Body	Flat Gold Tinsel or Mylar.
Under-	
Wing	Fox Squirrel Tail.
Overwing	Yellow Turkey Quill Segments.
Head	Spun Natural Gray Deer Hair clipped to shape leaving several strands extending toward bend.

White Maribou Muddler

Hook	Mustad 38941 or Mustad 79580.
Size	2 to 10
Thread	White - Pre-Waxed Monocord.
Tail	Red Hackle Fibers.
Body	Silver Tinsel Chenille.
Wing	White Maribou.
Topping	2 to 4 pieces of Peacock Herl.
Head	Spun Natural Gray Deer Hair clipped to shape leaving several strands extending toward bend.

Black Ghost

Hook	Mustad 9575
Size	2 to 10
Thread	Black
Tail	Yellow Hackle Fibers.
Body	Black Floss
Rib	Flat Silver Tinsel.
Beard	Yellow Hackle Fibers
Wing	White Saddle Hackle or Maribou.

Maribou Streamer

Hook	Mustad 9575
Size	2 to 10
Thread	Black
Body	Fine Silver Mylar Piping.
Wing	Yellow Maribou Over Red Bucktail.
Topping	Several Strands of Peacock Herl.
Note	Alternate Maribou Wing Colors May be Tied - Black is Good.

Matuka Sculpin

Hook	Mustad 38941 or 9672
Size	2 to 6
Thread	Amber
Rib	Fine Oval Gold Tinsel.
Body	Light Amber Sparkle Yarn.
Wing	Speckled Hen Saddle Hackle
Pectoral Fins	Speckled Hen Body Feather.
Head	Spun Deer Hair Clipped to Shape.
Note	See Page 186 for Tying Instructions.

Giz Leech

Hook	Mustad 79580 (Bend to Shape)
Size	2 to 10
Thread	Brown
Tail	Brown Maribou.
Body	Brown Sparkle Yarn.
Note	Alternate Colors May be Tied - Black is Very Good. See Page 190 for Tying Instructions.

Threadfin Shad

Hook	Mustad 9672
Size	2 to 10
Thread	Gray
Tail	Grizzly Marabou
Body	Braided Mylar Tubing Slipped Over Hook and Secured at Each End.
Note:	Silver or gold mylar may be used. Paint the back gray or black and coat the entire body with clear epoxy.

Black Leech

Hook	Mustad 33620
Size	4 to 10
Thread	Black - A Flat Waxed.
Tail	Black Marabou
Wing	Several Bunches of Black Marabou Tied on Top of Hook.
Body	Formed When Tying in the Wing Bunches with the Tying Thread.

Dave's Sculpin

Hook	Mustad 9672
Size	2 to 10
Thread	White
Body	Golden Ultratranslucent Dubbing.
Rib	Oval Gold Tinsel.
Wing	Furnace Hackle Tied Matuka Style.
Pectoral Fins	Yellow Dyed Grizzly Hen.
Head & Collar	Alternate Bunches of Black, Tan and Golden Brown Spun Deer Hair.

Golden Marabou Muddler

Hook	Mustad 9672
Size	2 to 10
Thread	Yellow
Tail	Golden Pheasant Tippet.
Body	Gold Oval Tinsel.
Wing	Yellow Marabou.
Head & Collar	Golden Yellow Spun Deer Hair.

Black Rabbit Streamer

Hook   Orvis 1526.
Size   2 to 10.
Thread   Black.
Body   Black Mylar Braid.
Wing   Black Rabbit Strip.

Pearl Rabbit Streamer

Hook   Orvis 1526.
Size   2 to 10.
Thread   Black.
Body   Pearlescent Mylar Braid.
Wing   White Rabbit Strip.
Hackle   Red.

Downwing Dry Flies

Marabou Leech

Hook   Orvis 1645.
Size   2 to 10.
Thread   Black.
Tail   Black Marabou and Pearl Mylar.
Wing   Black Marabou tied on top of hook in 3 or 4 places. Several long strands of Pearl Mylar should be tied in at head.

Wooly Bomber

Hook   Orvis 1526.
Size   2 to 12.
Thread   Black.
Tail   Black Marabou.
Body   Black Chenille Palmered with Grizzly Hackle.
Eyes   Lead Eyes painted Black with Yellow Pupils.
Note: Also works well in olive.

Wooly Bugger

Hook	Orvis 1526 - Inverted.
Size	2 to 10.
Thread	Black.
Body	Olive Furry Foam Palmed with Olive Hackle.
Wing	Pearlescent Flashabou over Olive Marabou over Olive Bucktail or Goat Hair.

Bucktail Muddler

Hook	Orvis 1526 - Inverted.
Size	2 to 12
Thread	Black.
Body	Pearlescent Body Flash.
Wing	Peacock Herl over Black Bucktail over Pearlescent Flashabou over Brown Bucktail.
Collar	Elk Body Hair.
Head	Spun Deer Body Hair.
Eyes	Doll Eyes.

Steelhead Flies

Single Egg Fly

Hook	Mustad 9174
Size	2 to 10
Thread	Red or White A Flat Waxed Thread.
Egg	Glo Bugs™ Yarn in any Combination of Colors.
Note	See Page 188 for Tying Instructions.

Boss

Hook	Eagle Claw 1197 or equivalent.
Size	2 to 8
Thread	Red - Pre-Waxed Monocord.
Tail	Gray Squirrel Tail dyed Black.
Rib	Flat Silver Tinsel or Mylar.
Body	Black Wool.
Hackle	Orange - Collar Style.
Eyes	Bead Chain Links tied on at head.

Black Prince

Hook	Eagle Claw 1197 or equivalent.
Size	2 to 8
Thread	Black - Pre-Waxed Monocord.
Tail	Red Hackle Fibers.
Rib	Oval Silver Tinsel.
Body	Rear 1/3 Yellow Floss. Front 2/3 Black Chenille.
Hackle	Black - Collar Style.
Wing	Black Calf Tail or Gray Squirrel Tail dyed Black.

Golden Demon

Hook	Eagle Claw 1197 or equivalent.
Size	2 to 8
Thread	Black - Pre-Waxed Monocord.
Tail	Golden Pheasant Crest Fibers.
Body	Oval Gold Tinsel.
Hackle	Orange - Collar Style.
Wing	Natural Brown Bucktail and Gray Squirrel Tail dyed Black mixed.

Purple Peril

Hook	Eagle Claw 1197 or equivalent.
Size	2 to 8
Thread	Black - Pre-Waxed Monocord.
Tail	Purple Hackle Fibers.
Rib	Oval Silver Tinsel.
Body	Purple Floss.
Hackle	Purple - Collar Style.
Wing	Natural Brown Bucktail.

Skunk

Hook	Eagle Claw 1197 or equivalent.
Size	2 to 8
Thread	Black - Pre-Waxed Monocord.
Tail	Red Hackle Fibers.
Rib	Oval Silver Tinsel.
Body	Black Chenille.
Hackle	Black - Collar Style.
Wing	White Bucktail or Calf Tail.

Skyomish Sunrise

Hook	Eagle Claw 1197 or equivalent.
Size	2 to 8
Thread	White - Pre-Waxed Monocord.
Tail	Red and Yellow Hackle Fibers mixed.
Rib	Flat Silver Tinsel or Mylar.
Body	Red Chenille.
Hackle	Red and Yellow mixed - Collar Style.
Wing	White Bucktail or Calf Tail.

Thor

Hook	Eagle Claw 1197 or equivalent.
Size	2 to 8
Thread	Black - Pre-Waxed Monocord.
Tail	Orange Hackle Fibers.
Body	Claret Chenille.
Hackle	Coachman Brown - Collar Style.
Wing	White Bucktail or Calf Tail.

Umpqua Special

Hook	Eagle Claw 1197 or equivalent.
Size	2 to 8
Thread	Red - Pre-Waxed Monocord.
Tail	White Bucktail or Calf Tail.
Rib	Flat Silver Tinsel or Mylar.
Body	Rear 1/3 Yellow Wool. Front 2/3 Red Wool.
Wing	White Bucktail over Red Bucktail over White Bucktail.
Hackle	Coachman Brown - Collar Style.

Polar Shrimp

Hook	Orvis 1645.
Size	2 to 8.
Thread	Black.
Tail	Red Hackle Fibers.
Body	Fluorescent Orange Chenille.
Hackle	Fluorescent Orange.
Wing	White Calf Tail.

Fall Favorite

Hook	Orvis 1645.
Size	2 to 8
Thread	Black.
Body	Silver Mylar Tinsel.
Hackle	Claret.
Wing	Orange Calf Tail.

Green Butt Skunk

Hook	Orvis 1645.
Size	2 to 8.
Thread	Black.
Tail	Red Hackle Fibers.
Butt	Fluorescent Green Chenille.
Body	Black Chenille.
Rib	Silver Mylar
Hackle	Black.
Wing	White Calf Tail.

Max Canyon (Umpqua)

Hook	Orvis 1645.
Size	2 to 8.
Thread	Black.
Tail	Orange over White Hackle Fibers.
Body	1/2 Fluorescent Orange Wool.
	1/2 Black Wool.
Rib	Silver Mylar.
Hackle	Black.
Wing	White over Orange Calf Tail.

Rubber Legs

Hook	Orvis 1511.
Size	2 to 8.
Thread	Fire Orange.
Tail	Orange Rubber Legs.
Body	Fluorescent Orange Chenille.
Legs	Orange Rubber Legs.
Feelers	Orange Rubber Legs.
Note:	Also works well in all Black or Chartreuse.

Goddard Caddis

Hook	Orvis 1644.
Size	4 to 10.
Thread	Brown.
Body	Spun Deer Body Hair Clipped to Shape.
Hackle	Brown.
Feelers	Brown Stripped Hackle Quills.

Babine Special

Hook	Orvis 1645.
Size	4 to 8.
Thread	Black.
Tail	White Marabou.
Body	Fluorescent Orange Chenille Tied in Two Balls Divided by a Red Hackle.
Hackle	White.

Greased Liner

Hook	Orvis 1644.
Size	4 to 10.
Thread	Black.
Tail	Deer Body Hair.
Body	Dark Brown Dubbing.
Hackle	Grizzly.
Wing	Deer Body Hair.
Head	Formed by Clipping Wing Butt.

Torrish

Hook	Mustad 36890
Size	2 to 10
Thread	Black
Tail	Golden Pheasant Crest.
Body	Embossed Silver Tinsel.
Rib	Palmered Yellow Hackle.
Throat	Guinea Hackle.
Wing	Black Bear or Squirrel.

Night Hawk

Hook	Mustad 36890
Size	2 to 10
Thread	Red
Tag	Fine Oval Gold Tinsel.
Tail	Blue Hackle Fibers Over Golden Pheasant Crest.
Butt	Fluorescent Orange Floss.
Body	Flat Silver Tinsel.
Rib	Fine Silver Tinsel.
Wing	Black Bear or Squirrel.
Topping	Golden Pheasant Crest.

Hairy Mary Tube

Hook	Straight Eye Double or Treble.
Size	2 to 10
Thread	Black
Body	1 inch to 3 inch Polyethylene Tube Covered with Black Floss and a Fine Flat Silver Tinsel Rib.
Wing	Gray Squirrel Tail Dyed Blue Mixed with Fox Squirrel.

Gary Tube

Hook	Straight Eye Double or Treble.
Size	2 to 10
Thread	Black
Body	1 inch to 3 inch Polyethylene Tube Covered with Black Floss and a Fine Flat Tinsel Rib.
Wing	Gray Squirrel Tail Dyed Red and Yellow Mixed.

Black Rat

Hook	Orvis Single or Double Salmon.
Size	2 to 10
Thread	Black - Pre-Waxed Monocord.
Tag	Flat Silver Tinsel or Mylar.
Body	Peacock Herl - Tied Full.
Wing	Gray Fox Guard Hairs.
Throat	Grizzly Hen - Collar Style.

Black Bear - Green Butt

Hook	Orvis Single or Double Salmon.
Size	2 to 10.
Thread	Black - Pre-Waxed Monocord.
Tag	Flat Silver Tinsel.
Tail	Gray Squirrel dyed Black.
Butt	Fluorescent Green Floss.
Rib	Flat Silver Tinsel.
Body	Black Floss.
Throat	Gray Squirrel dyed Black.
Wing	Gray Squirrel dyed Black.

Rusty Rat

Hook	Orvis Single or Double Salmon.
Size	2 to 10
Thread	Black - Pre-Waxed Monocord.
Tag	Oval Gold Tinsel.
Tail	Peacock Sword Fibers tied short.
Body	Rear Half Yellowish Orange Floss, Front Half Peacock Herl. A strand of floss extends over rear half of of body on the top of fly as a veil.
Wing	Gray Fox Guard Hairs.
Throat	Grizzly Hen - Collar Style.

Silver Rat

Hook	Orvis Single or Double Salmon.
Size	2 to 10.
Thread	Black - Pre-Waxed Monocord.
Rib	Oval Silver Tinsel.
Body	Flat Silver Tinsel or Mylar.
Wing	Gray Fox Guard Hairs.
Throat	Grizzly Hen - Collar Style.
Tag	Flat Silver Tinsel.

Hairy Mary

Hook	Orvis Single or Double Salmon.
Size	2 to 10
Thread	Black - Pre-Waxed Monocord.
Tag	Flat Gold Tinsel or Mylar.
Tail	Golden Pheasant Crest.
Rib	Flat Gold Tinsel or Mylar.
Body	Black Floss.
Throat	Bright Blue - Collar Style.
Wing	Reddish Brown Fitch Tail or Fox Squirrel Tail.

Hot Orange

Hook	Orvis Single or Double Salmon.
Size	2 to 10
Thread	Black - Pre-Waxed Monocord.
Tag	Flat Gold Tinsel or Mylar.
Tip	Yellow Floss.
Tail	Golden Pheasant Crest.
Rib	Flat Gold Tinsel or Mylar.
Body	Black Floss.
Throat	Bright Orange - Collar Style.
Wing	Gray Squirrel Tail dyed Black.

Cosseboom

Hook	Orvis Single or Double Salmon.
Size	2 to 10
Thread	Red - Pre-Waxed Monocord.
Tag	Flat Silver Tinsel or Mylar.
Tail	Olive Green Floss - cut short.
Rib	Flat Silver Tinsel.
Body	Olive Green Floss.
Wing	Gray Squirrel Tail.
Throat	Bright Yellow - Collar Style.

Roger's Fancy

Hook	Orvis Single or Double Salmon.
Size	2 to 10
Thread	Black - Pre-Waxed Monocord.
Tag	Oval Silver Tinsel.
Tip	Fluorescent Green Floss.
Tail	Peacock Sword Fibers - cut short.
Rib	Oval Silver Tinsel.
Body	Green Highlander African Goat.
Throat	Bright Green over Bright Yellow Hackle Fibers.
Wing	Badger Guard Hairs.

Engle's Butterfly

Hook	Orvis Single or Double Salmon.
Size	6 to 10
Thread	Black - Pre-Waxed Monocord.
Tag	Flat Gold Tinsel or Mylar.
Tail	Red Hackle Fibers.
Body	Peacock Herl.
Wing	White Calf Tail slightly longer than body, set on top of hook - Divided and Slanted backwards at a 45° angle.
Throat	Brown Hen - Collar Style.

Sweep

Hook	Orvis Single or Double Salmon.
Size	2 to 10
Thread	Black - Pre-Waxed Monocord.
Tag	Flat Gold Tinsel or Mylar.
Tail	Golden Pheasant Crest Fibers.
Rib	Flat Gold Tinsel or Mylar.
Throat	Black Hen - Collar Style.
Wing	Dyed Black Goose Quill Segment.
Cheek	Blue Kingfisher or Hen Hackle tip dyed appropriate color.
Body	Black Floss.

Salmon Muddler Minnow

Hook	Orvis Single or Double Salmon.
Size	2 to 10
Thread	Black - Pre-Waxed Monocord.
Tail	Mottled Turkey Quill Segments.
Body	Flat Gold Tinsel or Mylar.
Under-Wing	Gray Squirrel Tail.
Overwing	Mottled Turkey Quill Segments.
Head	Spun Natural Gray Deer Hair clipped to shape leaving several strands extended toward bend.

Blue Charm

Hook	Orvis Single or Double Salmon.
Size	2 to 10
Thread	Black - Pre-Waxed Monocord.
Tag	Flat Silver Tinsel or Mylar.
Tip	Yellow Floss.
Tail	Golden Pheasant Crest.
Rib	Flat Silver Tinsel or Mylar.
Body	Black Floss.
Throat	Deep Blue - Collar Style.
Wing	Turkey Tail Segments, veiled with Overwing of Teal along upper edge.
Topping	Golden Pheasant Crest.

Silver Doctor (Reduced)

Hook	Single or Double Salmon
Size	2 to 10
Tip	Flat Silver Tinsel.
Tag	Yellow Floss.
Tail	Golden Pheasant Crest.
Butt	Red Ostrich Herl.
Body	Flat Silver Tinsel.
Wing	Brown over Blue over Red over Yellow Calftail.
Throat	Kingfisher Blue Hackle Collar Style Pulled Down.
Beard	Guinea Hackle.

Black Dose (Reduced)

Hook	Single or Double Salmon
Size	2 to 10
Thread	Black
Tip	Flat Silver Tinsel.
Tag	Yellow Floss.
Tail	Golden Pheasant Crest.
Body	Black Floss.
Rib	Flat Silver Tinsel.
Wing	Black Bear or Squirrel Tail over Peacock Sword Fibers.
Hackle	Black Tied Collar Style.

Jock Scott (Reduced)

Hook	Single or Double Salmon
Size	2 to 10
Thread	Black
Tip	Flat Silver Tinsel.
Tag	Yellow Floss.
Tail	Golden Pheasant Crest.
Butt	Black Ostrich Herl.
Body	Rear 1/2 - Yellow Floss, Front 1/2 - Black African Goat.
Rib	Flat Silver Tinsel.
Wing	Yellow, Red and Blue Calftail Mixed over Peacock Sword over Brown Calftail.
Throat	Black Hackle Collar Style Pulled Down.

Dusty Miller (Reduced)

Hook	Single or Double Salmon
Size	2 to 10
Thread	Black
Tip	Flat Silver Tinsel.
Tag	Yellow Floss.
Tail	Amberst Pheasant Crest over Golden Pheasant Crest.
Butt	Black Ostrich Herl.
Body	Rear 1/2 Flat Silver Tinsel - Front 1/2 - Yellow Floss.
Rib	Flat Silver Tinsel.
Wing	Blue over Red over Yellow Calftail over Peacock Sword over Brown Calftail.
Throat	Green Highlander Hackle Collar Style and Pulled Down.
Beard	Guinea Hackle.

Silver Downeaster

Hook	Single or Double Salmon
Size	2 to 10
Thread	Black
Tag	Fine Oval Silver Tinsel.
Tail	Golden Pheasant Crest.
Butt	Black Ostrich Herl.
Body	Flat Silver Tinsel.
Rib	Fine Oval Silver Tinsel.
Collar	Orange Hackle - Collar Style Pulled Down.
Wing	Black Bear.

Undertaker

Hook	Single or Double Salmon
Size	2 to 10
Thread	Red
Butt	1/2 Fluorescent Green Wool - 1/2 Fluorescent Red Wool. End of Butt Should be Even with Hook Point.
Body	Peacock Herl.
Rib	Fine Oval Gold Tinsel.
Throat	Black Hackle.
Wing	Black Bear.

Green Highlander (Reduced)

Hook	Single or Double Salmon
Size	2 to 10
Thread	Black
Tip	Fine Flat Silver Tinsel.
Tag	Yellow Floss.
Tail	Golden Pheasant Crest.
Butt	Black Ostrich Herl.
Body	Rear 2/3 Yellow Floss - Front 1/3 Green Highlander African Goat.
Rib	Flat Silver Tinsel.
Throat	Green Highlander and Yellow Hackle - Collar Style and Pulled Down.
Wing	Oak Turkey or Substitute.

Blue Rat

Hook	Single or Double Salmon
Size	2 to 10
Thread	Red
Tag	Fine Oval Gold Tinsel.
Tail	Peacock Sword.
Body	2/3 Kingfisher Blue Floss - 1/3 Peacock Herl - A Strand of Floss Extends over the Rear 2/3 of the Body as a Veil.
Rib	Fine Oval Gold Tinsel.
Wing	Gray Fox Guard Hairs.
Throat	Grizzly Hackle Collar Style Pulled Down.
Cheek	Hen Hackle Dyed Kingfisher Blue.

Royal Wulff

Hook	Orvis Salmon Dry Fly.
Size	4 to 10
Thread	Black - Pre-Waxed Monocord.
Wing	White Calf Tail - Upright and Divided.
Tail	Brown Bucktail.
Body	Peacock Herl with a Red Floss Center Band.
Hackle	Coachman Brown - Tied Full.

White Wulff

Hook	Orvis Salmon Dry Fly.
Size	4 to 10
Thread	Black - Pre-Waxed Monocord.
Wing	White Calf Tail - Upright and Divided.
Tail	White Bucktail.
Body	Cream Colored Wool or Angora.
Hackle	Badger - Tied Full.

Salmon Irresistible

Hook	Orvis Salmon Dry Fly.
Size	4 to 10
Thread	Black - Pre-Waxed Monocord.
Tail	Natural Brown Bucktail.
Body	Spun Natural Gray Deer Hair clipped to shape.
Wing	Natural Brown Bucktail.
Hackle	Brown and Grizzly mixed - Tied Full.

Buck Bug

Hook	Orvis Salmon Dry Fly.
Size	4 to 10
Thread	Black - Pre-Waxed Monocord.
Tail	Fox Squirrel Tail.
Rib	Brown Saddle Hackle Palmered through body.
Body	Spun Natural Gray Deer Hair clipped to shape.
Hackle	Brown - Tied Full.

Shad Dart (Typical)

Hook	Mustad 3906B
Size	4 to 8
Thread	Orange
Tail	Orange Maribou.
Body	Orange Floss.
Rib	Flat Silver Tinsel.
Head	Orange Chenille.
Note	Alternate Color Combinations May Be Tied.

Connecticut River

Hook	Mustad 3906B
Size	4 to 8
Thread	Red
Tail	Red Goose or Turkey Quill.
Body	Flat Silver Tinsel.
Wing	Red Goose or Turkey Quill.
Note	Fly is Often Fished With a Red Bead Ahead of the Fly on the Tippet.

Narragansett Bay

Hook	Mustad 38941
Size	4 to 8
Thread	Gray
Tail	Golden Pheasant Crest.
Body	Gray Sparkle Yarn.
Rib	Flat Gold Tinsel.
Wing	Green over Gray Bucktail.
Eyes	Red.

Chesapeake Bay

Hook	Mustad 38941
Size	4 to 8
Thread	White
Tail	Golden Pheasant Crest.
Body	White Sparkle Yarn.
Rib	Flat Silver Tinsel.
Wing	White Bucktail.
Eyes	Red.

Keel Bass Bug

Hook	Eagle Claw No. 1213
Size	2 to 6
Thread	Red
Tail	Red Inside Yellow Hackle Tips.
Body	Green Deer Body Hair Tied Parallel to and Surrounding Hook Shank.
Wing	Gray Squirrel Tail.
Head	Green Deer Body Hair Spun and Clipped to Shape. Flat on Bottom and Top leaving several strands on Top extending over Wing.
Note	Alternate Color Combinations May be Tied. Yellow is especially effective.

Bass Getter - Basic Hair Bug

Hook	Mustad 7957B
Size	1/0 to 4
Thread	White
Weed Guard	.019 Monofilament.
Legs	Rubber.
Tail	Rubber inside Yellow Maribou Inside 4 White Saddle Hackles Splayed.
Body	Black, Yellow and White Deer Body Hair Spun and Clipped to Shape.
Note	See Page 189 for Tying Instructions. Alternate Color Combinations May be tied.

Maribou Leech

Hook	Salmon Single or Mustad 9672
Size	1/0 to 4
Weed Guard	.019 Monofilament.
Thread	Black
Tail	Black Maribou.
Body	Black Sparkle Yarn.
Rib	Palmered Black Saddle Hackle.
Eyes	Bead Chain
Note	Alternate Color Combinations May be Tied. Olive in Size 6 works well for Trout.

Maribou Matuka

Hook	Mustad 38941
Size	1/0 to 4
Weed Guard	.019 Monofilament.
Thread	White
Body	Gold Sparkle Yarn.
Wing	Brown Ostrich over Gold Mylar Tinsel over Gold Maribou Tied in Matuka Style.
Rib	Fine Oval Gold Tinsel.
Shoulders	Teal Flank Dyed Gold and Lacquered.
Eyes	Yellow Enamel with Black Pupils.
Note	Alternate Color Combinations May be Tied.

Peeper Popper

Hook	Mustad 33900
Size	2 to 10
Body	Cork sanded to shape and painted desired color. Mounting hook to cork may be found in Index Supplement I, Page 15.
Tail	Desired Color Hackle Tips.
Hackle	Color as Desired.
Note:	Rubber Legs may be pulled thru cork body with a sewing needle.

Sneaky Pete

Hook	Mustad 33900.
Size	2 to 10.
Body	Cork sanded to shape and painted desired color.
Tail	Fluorescent Floss and Rubber Legs.
Hackle	Color as Desired.

Kicker Frog

Hook	Orvis 0520
Size	1/0 to 6
Legs	Green over Yellow Bucktail. A short piece of wire is tied in the middle of the leg with tying thread then bent to shape.
Body	Green Spun Deer Body Hair on top and Yellow Spun Deer Body Hair on bottom.
Eyes	Doll Eyes or Dab of Latex Caulking Painted.

Gerbubble Bug

Hook	Orvis 0520.
Size	1/0 to 6.
Tail	Four Hackle Tips.
Body	Spun Deer Body Hair.
Legs	Formed by pulling hackle butts from tails forward along sides of body working the quills into the body and tying off at head.
Note:	Pattern can be tied in any color combination.

Perch Prismatic Muddler

Hook	Mustad 79580
Size	1/0 to 4
Thread	White
Body	Gold Prismatic Mylar.
Wing	Green Marabou with Green Dyed Grizzly Hackle Tied on the Sides.
Head & Collar	Olive Spun Deer Hair Over Yellow Spun Deer Hair.
Eyes	Plastic Doll Eyes.

Prismatic Shiner

Hook	Mustad 9672
Size	1/0 to 6
Thread	White
Body	Silver Prismatic Mylar.
Wing	White Marabou.
Topping	Purple Ostrich Over Olive Ostrich.
Eyes	Plastic Doll Eyes.

Silver Prismatic Muddler

Hook	Mustad 79580
Size	1/0 to 4
Thread	White
Body	Silver Prismatic Mylar.
Wing	White Marabou with Natural Grizzly Hackle Tied on the Sides.
Head & Collar	Natural Gray Spun Deer Hair Over Natural White Spun Deer Hair.
Eyes	Plastic Doll Eyes.

Floating Marabou Muddler

Hook	Mustad 79580
Size	1/0 to 4
Thread	White
Body	Silver Mylar Tubing.
Wing	Black, White or Yellow Marabou with Silver Mylar Tied on the Sides.
Topping	Peacock Herl.
Head & Collar	White Spun Deer Hair on Bottom, Natural on Sides and Olive on Top.

Diving Bug

Hook	Orvis 0520.
Size	1/0 to 6.
Tail	Desired color Flashabou over Marabou.
Body	Deer body hair spun and clipped to shape. Top should be clipped leaving a fan shape collar twice the diameter of the head. Deer hair behind the collar should be left unclipped extending back over tail. Collar should be coated with "Flexament."

Rabbit Strip Diver

Hook	Mustad 3366.
Size	1/0 to 6.
Tail	Rabbit Fur Strip.
Body	Formed by winding tail material around hook shank and clipping on bottom and sides.
Topping	Several strands of Flashabou.
Head	Spun Deer Body Hair clipped to shape as in Diving Bug.

Flashdancer

Hook	Mustad 3366.
Size	1/0 to 6.
Tail	Red Marabou.
Body	White Chenille.
Wing	Pearlescent Flashabou.
Head	Spun Deer Body Hair clipped to shape.

Slider

Hook	Mustad 3366.
Size	1/0 to 6.
Tail	Flashabou 1/2 length of wing.
Wing	Rabbit Fur Strip.
Sides	Grizzly Hackle Tips.
Head	Spun Deer Body Hair clipped to shape.
Note:	Black and White are good producers.

Bass Flies   **149**

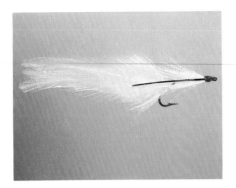

Lefty's Deceiver

Hook	Mustad 34007.
Size	3/0 to 2
Thread	Red - Pre-Waxed Monocord.
Tail	4 White Saddle Hackles not splayed.
Body	Flat Silver Mylar.
Hackle	White Bucktail or Calf Tail, tied as a collar - extending to the hook point.
Cheek	Strips of Mylar extending past bend of hook.

Sand Eel

Hook	Mustad 34007.
Size	Leading Hook 3/0 to 1/0 - Trailing Hook 1/0 to 2.
Thread	Red - Pre-Waxed Monocord.
Tail	End of Mylar Piping Body picked out.
Body	Silver Mylar Piping.
Wing	Badger Saddle Hackles tied down at bend of Trailing Hook.
Throat	Peacock Sword Fibers.
Eyes	Lacquered Black with Yellow Dot.
Note	See page 191 for Tying Instructions.

Gibb's Striper

Hook	Mustad 34007.
Size	3/0 to 2
Thread	Black - Pre-Waxed Monocord.
Body	Flat Silver Mylar.
Wing	White Bucktail.
Cheek	Jungle Cock Hackle over a slip of Goose or Turkey Quill dyed blue.
Throat	Red Hackle Fibers.
Eyes	Lacquered Yellow with Red Dot.

Glass Minnow

Hook	Mustad 34007.
Size	1/0 to 2
Thread	Black - Pre-Waxed Monocord.
Body	Clear Flat Mono over Flat Silver Mylar.
Wing	Green Bucktail over White Bucktail.
Cheek	Strips of Mylar extending 3/4 length of wing.
Eyes	Lacquered Yellow with Black Dot.

Red/Yellow Deceiver

Hook	Mustad 34007.
Size	5/0 to 6.
Thread	Red.
Tail	Yellow Bucktail inside 4 Yellow Neck Hackles.
Body	Silver Mylar Tinsel.
Collar	Red Bucktail or Calf Tail spread evenly around hook shank to form collar.
Topping	Peacock Herl over Silver Nylon Tinsel or Crystal Flash.

Orvis Optic Deceiver

Hook	Orvis Optic Deceiver.
Size	2/0 or 2.
Thread	Desired Color.
Tail	4 Neck Hackles of Desired Color.
Collar	Bucktail or Calf Tail of Desired Color or spread evenly around hook shank to form collar.
Cheeks	Desired color Crystal Flash.

Sea-Ducer

Hook	Mustad 34007.
Size	5/0 to 4.
Thread	Red.
Tail	Mylar Tinsel or Crystal Flash over 4 Neck Hackles splayed out.
Body	Palmered Saddle Hackle.
Collar	Different Color Saddle Hackle than Body.

Bend Back

Hook	Mustad 34007.
Size	5/0 to 4.
Note:	Bend hook spand down at a 15° angle. 1/3 shank length behind eye.
Body	Silver/Gold or Pearlescent Mylar Tinsel.
Wing	Bucktail of desired color.
Topping	Mylar Tinsel, Crystal Flash or Peacock Herl if desired.

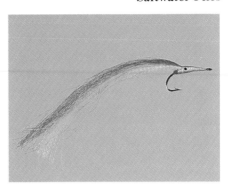

Silver Sides

Hook   Mustad 92608.
Size   2 to 6.
Tail   Olive Marabou.
Body   Mylar Braid pulled over body form, painted and epoxied.
Body Form Cut 2 pieces of plastic with serrated scissors to desired shape. Tie in tightly on each side of hook shank.

Needlefish

Hook   Mustad 34007.
Size   5/0 to 2.
Thread   Fluorescent Lime Floss.
Tail   Dark Green Fishair over Fluorescent Green Fishair over White Crinkle Nylon.
Tag   Red Sparkle Yarn.
Butt   Light Green Sparkle Yarn.
Head   Fluorescent Lime Floss.
Note: Sparkle Yarn can be Antron® Yarn or Aunt Lydia's Rug Yarn.

Finger Mullet

Hook   Mustad 34007.
Size   3/0 to 1/0
Thread   White.
Eyes   Nickel Plated Lead Eyes.
Tail   Grizzly Neck Hackle.
Body   Rear 1/5 — Spun Antelope Body Hair. Front — Spun White Deer Body Hair clipped to shape.
Note: Also works well with Red Tail and Yellow Body.

Redfish

Hook   Mustad 34007.
Size   2/0 to 2.
Thread   Fluorescent Red Floss.
Tail   White Neck Hackle Splayed Out inside Silver Mylar Tinsel or Crystal Flash.
Collar   Red Marabou wound Hackle Style and clipped to length.

Bonefish Leech (Typical)

Hook Mustad 34007
Size 2 to 8
Thread Yellow
Tail White over Yellow Maribou.
Body Yellow Acrylic Yarn Tied Flat.

Note Alternate Color Combinations May Be Tied. Pink is Especially Effective. See Page 190 for Tying Instructions.

Permit Fly

Hook Mustad 34007
Size 1/0 to 4
Thread Tan
Tail Badger Guard Hairs Inside Furnace Hackle.
Hackle Furnace.
Body Tan Chenille.
Eyes Amber Glass.

Blue Death Tarpon

Hook Mustad 34007
Size 5/0 to 3/0
Thread Fluorescent Pink.
Tail Blue Bucktail Inside Dark Blue Saddle Hackle Inside Grizzly Saddle Hackle.
Collar Dark Blue and Grizzly Saddle Mixed.

Skipping Bug (Typical)

Hook Mustad 33903 or Equivalent
Size 2/0
Tail White Bucktail.
Body 3 Inch Perch Float Cut in 1/2 and Painted.

Note See Page 192 for Tying Instructions.

Keys Tarpon

Hook	Mustad 34007.
Size	3/0 to 5/0.
Thread	Brown.
Tail	Orange Bucktail inside 4 Brown Neck Hackles Splayed Out.
Collar	Orange Marabou Wound Hackle Style
Head	Clear Body Glass or "V" Rib over Brown Thread.

Orange Tarpon

Hook	Mustad 34007.
Size	3/0 to 5/0.
Thread	Fire Orange.
Tail	Fox Squirrel Tail inside 2 Brown Neck Hackles inside 4 Orange Neck Hackles.
Cheeks	Cock Ringneck Pheasant Body Feathers.
Head	Fire Orange Tying Thread with Painted Eyes.

Deep Water Tarpon — Black

Hook	Mustad 34007.
Size	3/0 to 5/0.
Thread	Red.
Eyes	Glass Eyes — 8 mm.
Tail	Black Marabou over Red Marabou inside 4 Grizzly Saddle Hackles inside 4 Black Saddle Hackles.
Collar/ Head	Black Rabbit Strip Wound Around Hook Shank to Hook Eye. Clip Fur Short to Behind Eyes.

Deep Water Tarpon — Chartreuse

Hook	Mustad 34007.
Size	3/0 to 5/0.
Thread	Black.
Eyes	7 mm. Doll Eyes epoxied to 1/4-inch nickel-plated lead eyes.
Tail	Chartreuse Marabou over Pearlescent Crystal Flash inside 6 Chartreuse Saddle Hackles.
Collar/ Head	Chartreuse Rabbit Strip Wound Same as Deep Water Tarpon Black.

Apte Tarpon Fly

Hook   Mustad 34007.
Size   3/0 to 5/0.
Thread   Orange - Pre-Waxed Monocord.
Tail   2 Orange Saddle Hackles inside 4
           Yellow Saddle Hackles. Dull side
           of Hackles facing out (splayed).
Hackle   Webby Butt Ends of the Tail
           Saddle Hackles tied back trimming
           excess stem.

Chinese Claw

Hook   Mustad 34007.
Size   3/0 to 5/0.
Thread   Black - Pre-Waxed Monocord.
Tail   2 Yellow Saddle Hackles inside 4
           Grizzly Saddle Hackles. Dull side
           of Hackles facing out (splayed).
Hackle   Black and Grizzly Saddle Hackle
           mixed.

Hi-Ti

Hook   Mustad 34007.
Size   3/0 to 5/0
Thread   Orange - Pre-Waxed Monocord.
Tail   White Bucktail.
Wing   4 small clumps of White Bucktail
           tied progressively spaced up the
           hook shank toward the eye. The
           5th clump may be green, red, yel-
           low, orange or blue Bucktail tied
           in at the head.

Cockroach

Hook   Mustad 34007.
Size   3/0 to 5/0
Thread   Black - Pre-Waxed Monocord.
Wing   4 Grizzly Saddle Hackles tied
           shining side out.
Hackle   Natural Brown Bucktail tied as a
           collar extending to the hook
           point.

Orvis Bonefisher — Style 1

Hook   Orvis 1702 Bonefisher Body tinted
desired color with waterproof
marker.

Tail   Desired color Calf Tail or Squirrel
Tail

Soft Bonefish

Hook   Mustad 34007.

Size   1 to 4.

Thread To match color of fly.

Tail   Calf Tail inside 2 Hackle Tips.

Body   Form Diamond Shape by cutting two
thin pieces of stiff plastic with serrated scissors. Tie in on top and bottom of hook, then overwind with
floss of desired color. Tie in glass
eyes and coat body with Aqua-Seal.

Eyes   Glass Eyes — 4 mm.

Orvis Bonefisher — Style 2

Hook   Orvis 1702 Bonefisher body tinted
desired color with waterproof
marker.

Wing   Desired color Calf Tail or Squirrel
Tail.

Orvis Bonefisher — Style 3

Hook   Orvis 1702 Bonefisher Body tinted to
desired color with waterproof
marker.

Tail/   2 hackle tips splayed out. Tie in
Collar   hackle tips and wind butts of hackle
to form collar.

Sparkle Bonefish

Hook	Mustad 34007.
Size	2 to 8.
Thread	Yellow.
Eyes	Glass Eyes, 4 mm.
Body	Tan Antron® Dubbing with Pearl Crystal Flash Cut Up and Mixed with Dubbing.
Wing	Tan Calf Tail.

Boca Bonefish — Yellow

Hook	Mustad 34007.
Size	2 to 8.
Thread	Yellow.
Eyes	Glass Eyes — 4 mm.
Body	Yellow Antron® Dubbing.
Wing	Gray Squirrel Dyed Yellow.

Boca Bonefish — Tangerine

Hook	Mustad 34007.
Size	2 to 8.
Thread	Tan.
Eyes	Glass Eyes — 4 mm.
Body	Tan Antron® Dubbing.
Wing	Tangerine Calf Tail.
Note:	White Calf Tail may be dyed using RIT #40 Tangerine Dye.

Yellow Crazy Charlie

Hook	Mustad 34007.
Size	2 to 8.
Thread	Yellow.
Eyes	Nickel Plated Lead Eyes.
Body	Clear Body Glass or "V" Rib over Yellow Pearlescent Fly Flash Wing Material.
Wing	Yellow Calf Tail.

Canada Flats

Hook	Mustad 34007.
Size	2 to 8.
Thread	Black.
Eyes	Silver Bead Chain.
Body	Clear Body Glass or ''V'' Rib over Black Flashabou.
Wing	Pink Calf Tail.

Crazy Charlie #1

Hook	Mustad 34007.
Size	2 to 8.
Thread	White.
Eyes	Nickel Plated Lead Eyes.
Body	Clear Body Glass or ''V'' Rib over Pearlescent Tinsel.
Wing	4 Cream Hackle Tips splayed out.

Crazy Charlie #2

Hook	Mustad 34007.
Size	2 to 8.
Thread	White.
Eyes	Silver Bead Chain.
Body	Clear Body Glass or ''V'' Rib over Pearlescent Tinsel.
Wing	Tan Calf Tail.

Paris Flats

Hook	Mustad 34007.
Size	2 to 8.
Thread	Yellow.
Eyes	Silver Bead Chain.
Body	Tan Vernile.
Wing	Tan Calf Tail.
Head	Fluorescent Yellow Vernile.

Bonefish Crab

Hook	Mustad 94151.
Size	2 to 6.
Thread	Brown.
Tail	Brown Bucktail.
Body	Brown Chenille.
Eyes	Burned Back Monofilament.
Feelers	Brown Bucktail.

F.A. Bonefish

Hook	Mustad 34007.
Size	2 to 6.
Thread	Brown.
Wing	Pink Marabou over Orange Marabou over Fox Squirrel Tail.
Sides	Orange Grizzly Hackle Tips.

Horror

Hook	Mustad 34007.
Size	2 to 6.
Thread	Black.
Wing	Brown Hackle Tips over Natural Brown Bucktail.
Head	Yellow Chenille.

Rabbit Fur Bonefish

Hook	Mustad 34007.
Size	2 to 6.
Thread	Fire Orange.
Body	Desired Color Chenille.
Wing	Rabbit Fur Strip. Pierce hole in tail end of rabbit strip and slide over hook point around bend to back of body to secure.

Grass Shrimp

Hook	Mustad 34007
Size	2 to 8
Thread	Black
Body	Light Green Ultratranslucent Dubbing.
Wing	Light Blue Fishair Under Light Blue Grizzly Hackle Tips.

Brown Snapping Shrimp

Hook	Mustad 34007
Size	2 to 8
Thread	Black
Body	Rear 1/3 Rust and Front 2/3 Beige Ultratranslucent Dubbing.
Wing	Brown Fishair.

Golden Mantis Shrimp

Hook	Mustad 34007
Size	2 to 8
Thread	Red
Body	Fluorescent Green Chenille.
Wing	Golden Yellow Fishair Under Yellow Grizzly Hackle Tips.

Bonefish Special

Hook	Mustad 34007
Size	2 to 8
Thread	Black
Tail	Orange Marabou.
Body	Gold Mylar Overwrapped with Flat Mono.
Wing	White Fishair Under Natural Grizzly Hackle Tips.

Frankie-Belle

Hook	Mustad 34007 tied inverted.
Size	2 to 6
Thread	Red - Pre-Waxed Monocord.
Body	Fluorescent White Chenille.
Wing	White Bucktail or Calf Tail.
Cheek	Grizzly Hackle Tips - 3/4 length of Wing over which are tied Mylar Strips equal to the wing length.

Horror

Hook	Mustad 34007 tied inverted.
Size	2 to 6
Thread	Red - Pre-Waxed Monocord.
Wing	Natural Brown Bucktail tied at middle of hook shank.
Tag	Flat Silver Mylar.
Body	Fluorescent Orange Chenille tied short on each side of wing.

Pink Shrimp

Hook	Mustad 34007.
Size	2 to 6
Thread	White - Pre-Waxed Monocord.
Tail	Pink Hackle Fibers.
Back	Pink Bucktail pulled over body.
Rib	Pink Hackle Palmered through Body.
Body	Flat Silver Mylar.

Honey Blonde

Hook	Mustad 34007.
Size	3/0 to 4
Thread	Yellow - Pre-Waxed Monocord.
Tail	Yellow Bucktail or Calf Tail.
Body	Flat Gold Mylar.
Wing	Yellow Bucktail or Calf Tail.

PART III

Special
Fly-Tying
Instructions

Step 1.

Dub on a small fur ball at hook bend and wrap tying thread forward.

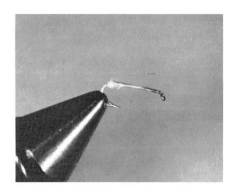

Step 2.

Tie in a bunch of hackle fibers on top of the hook shank. Wrap the tying thread toward the bend securing the hackle and dividing them into equal bunches on each side of the fur ball.

Instructions continued on page 166.

Step 3.

Select two matched mallard wing quill segments, 1 right and 1 left. The width of the segments should be equal to the width of the hook gap. Holding the wings by the tips, the butts should straddle the shank slanted back at a 60⁰ angle. Bring the tying thread up between the wings, down over the far wing, under the shank, up over the near wing, and again down over the far wing. Squeeze the wings tightly between the thumb and forefinger and pull the tying thread down to secure the wing. Take one or two additional wraps around the wing butts before removing pressure.

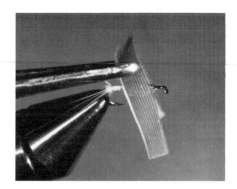

Step 4.

Clip off excess wing material and take 1 or 2 figure "8's" to divide the wings. Wrap tying thread to base of tail.

Step 5.

Dub body to base of wing, cross over the front of wing and tie off.

HAYSTACK

Step 1.

Tie in a bundle of deer, elk, moose or caribou hair extending over the eye of hook equal to the desired wing length.

Step 2.

Stand up wing by winding tying thread in front of the wing. The wing should be fan shaped and flat. Tie in a full tail.

Step 3.

Dub body to base of wing and take 1 or 2 turns of dubbing in front of wing. Tie off head.

Suggested Haystack Patterns

Haystacks may be tied in any combination of colors and are excellent fast water patterns. Small sizes are effective in flat water.

PATTERN	WING/TAIL	BODY
Dark	Natural Deer Hair	Dark Australian Opossum
Gray	Dyed Gray Deer Hair	Muskrat
Brown	Dyed Brown Deer Hair	Brown Fur or Poly
Mahogany	Moose Hair	Mahogany Fur or Poly
Olive	Dyed Dark Gray Deer Hair	Olive Fur or Poly

Step 1.

Tie in wings as in a Traditional divided wing Dry Fly except more widely divided, i. e. 90°. Hair Wings are preferred such as calf tail, moose, elk, deer or mink to provide a stable base to wind the hackle.

Tie in 2 hackles between the wings and extend over the eye.

Step 2.

Tie in tail and dub body. 1 turn of dubbing should be placed behind and in front of wing.

Step 3.

Wind hackle around base of each wing. Winding the hackle is done in the same manner as a Parachute Dry Fly. When the hackle is properly wound, the fibers will form an X between the wings.

Step 4.

Whip finish head. Waterwalkers are very stable and high floating flies in fast water.

See Page 193 for additional descriptions.

Step 1.

Tie in 2 or 3 fibers from a Ringneck Pheasant center tail and fine gold wire at the hook bend.

Step 2.

Grasp the center tail fibers in an E-Z hook hackle plier or similar tool and twist lightly. Wrap the twisted fibers toward the eye allowing for enough room to tie in the hackle and wing. Spiral the wire toward the eye in the opposite direction the body was wrapped.

Step 3.

Tie in a bunch of long stiff hackle fibers or mink tail guard hairs flat over body and slightly curving down along sides. Cut off excess wing material on a diagonal.

Step 4.

Tie in hackle and wind over wing butts. Tie off head.

Step 1.

Tie in one hackle perpendicular to the hook shank - half way between the eye and the hook point.

Step 2.

Wrap tying thread to the hook bend. Dub a tapered body toward the hook eye allowing for enough room to tie in the hackle and wing.

Step 3.

Wind hackle through thorax area and tie off. Clip the hackle on top and bottom.

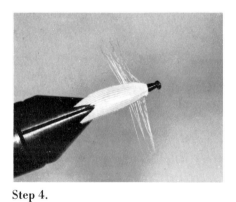

Step 4.

Spray a mallard or similar wing quill with a fixative such as Tuffilm. Cut a segment from the wing quill the appropriate length. Cut a "V" notch as shown in the photo. Tie in wing flat over body slightly curving down along sides. Cut off excess wing material on a diagonal and tie off head.

Step 1.

Wrap the tying thread to a point half way down the hook bend. Dub a tapered body ending slightly forward of the hook point.

Step 2.

Wrap the tying thread toward the eye. Tie in 4 dark moose body hairs on top of the hook. Wrap the thread toward the bend dividing the moose hairs on each side of the fur body.

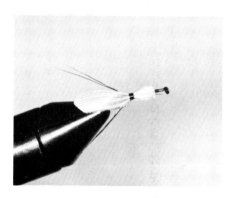

Step 3.

Spray a mallard wing quill with a fixative such as Tuffilm. Cut the mallard section to shape and tie in flat over back extending past the hook bend.

Step 4.

Tie in a hackle at the base of the wing and wind forward allowing for enough room for the front half of the body. Dub front section of body and tie off head.

Step 1.

Tie in tail, hackle rib and dub body. Tie in a sparse bucktail wing.

Step 2.

To make legs, spray a turkey or golden pheasant tail with Tuffilm. Cut a segment of the tail equal in width to the desired leg size. Tie an overhand knot in the tail segment using either tweezers or surgical forceps. Surgical forceps are much easier to use than tweezers since they can be locked closed. Pull the knot tight until the leg is bent at a 90° angle. Put a drop of vinyl or head cement on the knot.

Step 3.

Tie in a segment of turkey or golden pheasant tail that has been previously sprayed with Tuffilm, flat over the back, extending half the tail length past the bend of the hook. Tie in legs on the sides of the body and clip the tips to a desired length.

Step 4.

Spin deer hair head and allow several strands to extend back to hook point. Clip head to shape.

Note: This pattern also produces an effective cricket when tied in darker colors.

TYING THE BETTS EXTENDED BODY

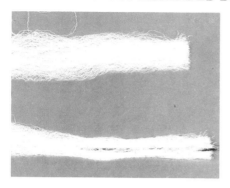

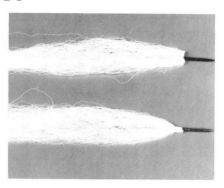

Step 1.

Cut a piece of polypropylene yarn three inches long. Comb the yarn so all the fibers are reasonably parallel. Take a number 5 or 6 needle and insert it eye first into the bundle of yarn. The yarn should be evenly distributed around the needle.

Step 2.

Melt the yarn back 1/8 inch from the needle point using a disposable butane lighter. While the end of the yarn is still soft, roll the yarn and needle between the thumb and forefinger to produce a round tapered bead as shown in the photo.

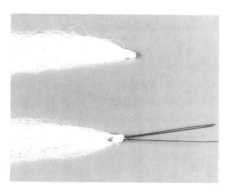

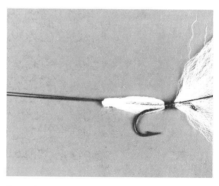

Step 3.

Remove the needle from the bundle of yarn: Insert two or three tail fibers such as micro-fibetts or another desired tailing material into the hole produced by the needle. Push the tail fibers through the yarn far enough so they may be bound to the hook shank.

Step 4.

Secure the yarn body and tails to the middle of the hook shank as shown.

Instructions continued on Page 174.

Special Fly-Tying Instructions   173

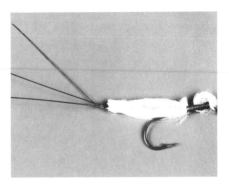

Step 5.
Pull excess body and tail material toward the bend of the hook and secure as shown in photo.

Step 6.
Clip excess yarn and tail material.

Note: Spinner wings or legs should be tied on the hook shank prior to tying in the extended body. Upright polyethylene wings and flat wing caddis and stonefly wings should be tied in after the extended body is secured to the hook shank.

The synthetic wings, body and tails may all be tinted with waterproof marking pens.

Step 1.

Wind tying thread to middle of hook. Secure a bundle of deer, moose, or elk hair on top of and parallel to hook shank.

Step 2.

Grasp bundle of hair by the tips and pull the fibers taut. Spiral tying thread toward tips and back to hook shank forming a tight bundle.

Step 3.

Clip excess hairs to form tails. Apply a light coating of head or vinyl cement over the body.

Note:

Many patterns of dry flies may be adapted to this technique by varying the body color and hackle and wing style. Suggested patterns are listed below.

PATTERN	OLIVE	GRAY	YELLOW	WHITE
Thread	Olive	Gray	Yellow	White
Tail/Body	Olive	Gray	Yellow	White
Wing * 1.	Med. Dun	Med. Dun	Wood Duck	Grizzly
Hackle * 2.	Med. Dun	Med. Dun	Ginger	Grizzly
Thorax * 3.	Olive Poly	Gray Poly	Yellow Poly	White Poly

* 1.   Colors specified for Duns — for Spinners use Light Dun Hen Hackle or Poly Wing material.
* 2.   May be tied in Traditional style or Parachute style.
* 3.   Required only when tying Spinner and Thorax patterns.

FUR EXTENDED BODY DRY FLY

Step 1.

Insert a very fine needle or wire in the vise. Cover the needle with tying thread equal to the length of the desired body, and leaving a strand 4 inches long extend toward the vise. Tie in a bundle of deer, moose or elk hair parallel to the needle and twice the length of the desired body.

Step 2.

Apply dubbing material to thread in the normal fashion. Take two turns of dubbing a-round the body and pull the strand of thread left hanging from the previous step over the two turns of dubbing. Wind the dubbing over the strand of thread to front of body, locking the thread under the dubbing. Whip finish and apply head cement.

Step 3.

Slide the completed body off the needle. Place the hook into the vise and wind the tying thread to the middle of the shank. Secure the body to the hook shank and apply a small amount of dubbing over the end of the body. Clip away ex-cess hair to form tail.

Note: Many patterns of dry flies, i. e. Thorax, Parachute, Spinner or Traditional may be adapted to this technique by varying the body color and wing and hackle styles.

See Page 193 for additional pattern descriptions.

Step 1.

Tie a small bunch of hackle fibers on top of the hook shank.
Wrap the thread, securing the
hackle fibers to a point 2 turns
down on hook bend. Take one
turn under the tail to splay the
hackle fibers. Tie in rib.

Step 2.

Dub body forward, allowing
for enough room for the wing
case and legs. Spiral the rib
through the body.

Step 3.

Apply a poly dubbing material
to the tying thread in the usual
manner. Raise the tying thread
above the shank and keep it
taught. Twist and slide the
dubbing down the thread to
form a ball on top of the shank.

**Instructions continued on
Page 178.**

FLOATING NYMPHS continued

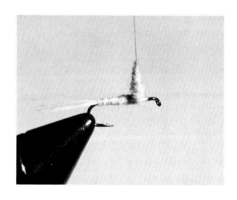

Step 4.

Hold the fur ball in position and take several turns around the hook shank and the base of the wing case to secure it to the hook shank.

Step 5.

Tie in a small bunch of hackle fibers on top of the hook shank in front of the wing case. Wrap the tying thread toward the wing case to secure the hackle fibers and divide them into equal bunches on each side of the wing case.

Step 6.

Dub a small amount of poly over the hackle butts close to the wing case and tie off.

FUR CADDIS PUPA

Step 1.

Wrap the tying thread to a point half way down the hook bend on a Mustad 3906 or to a point directly across from the barb on a Mustad 37160. Dub a tapered body toward the eye allowing for enough room to tie in the head.

Step 2.

Spray a right and left mallard quill with a fixative, Tuffilm is recommended. Tie in a small section of the mallard quill on each side of the body with the leading edge pointing down and with the natural curvature of the quill section toward the body.

Step 3.

Tie in a beard style hackle using the appropriate material. Dub the head and tie off.

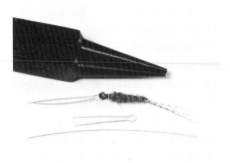

Step 1.

Place a ringed eye hook in vise. Wind tying thread toward the bend. Tie in tail on the side of hook shank. Dub body, tie off and lacquer head.

Step 2.

Remove hook from vise and cut hook off just under tail with wire cutters. Take a piece of fine stainless steel wire, .007 to .010 inches, and form a loop as shown in the photo using wire bending pliers or bend the wire around a needle. Slide nymph tail section onto wire.

Step 3.

Place hook in vise and wind tying thread to bend. Tie in wire holding the tail section on top of the hook shank.

Step 4.

Dub a small amount of fur on hook. Tie in wing case. Dub the remainder of the Thorax to just behind the eye. Tie in legs and pull wing case forward. Tie off and lacquer head.

See Page 194 for additional pattern descriptions.

FUR CADDIS PUPA

Step 1.

Dub body allowing enough room behind eye for head and legs. Spray mallard or speckled hen quills with Tuffilm. Tie in the segments along the sides of the body.

Step 2.

Spin red or gray squirrel guard hairs and underfur in a loop.

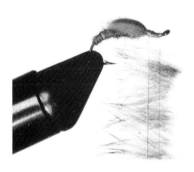

Step 3.

Wind spun dubbing around hook to form head. While winding the dubbing around head, wet your fingers and comb the fur toward the bend of the hook. Clip the fur from the top of the head even with the top of the body. Tie off and lacquer head.

See Page 194 for additional pattern descriptions.

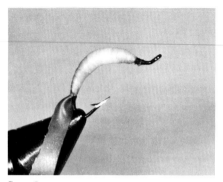

Step 1.

Tie in one strip of thin latex of the desired color and one strip of thick cream latex at the hook bend. Latex may be easily cut with scissors by placing the latex sheet between two pieces of paper. Wrap a tapered underbody using the thick latex. The body should be tapered at each end and heavier in the middle.

Step 2.

Wrap the thin latex of the appropriate color over the underbody. Tie in two mallard wing quill segments as described in the Fur Caddis Pupa tying instructions (on Page 181).

Step 3.

Tie in red or gray squirrel guard hairs including underfur encompassing the two sides and bottom of the body extending to the hook barb. The guard hairs and underfur may also be tied in by using the LOOP technique of dubbing and clipping the excess fur on top of the hook.

Step 4.

Dub fur head and tie off at eye.

Step 1.

Dub a small ball at bend of hook. Tie in one goose wing quill leading edge fiber on each side of hook and divide on each side of fur ball. Dub a tapered abdomen ending at the middle of the hook shank. Tie in the wing case.

Step 2.

Dub half the area in front of the wing case. Bend the wing case toward the bend of the hook. Fold the wing case forward and secure it in front of the thorax. Fold the remaining end of the wing case back and secure.

Step 3.

Dub the remaining area in front of the wing case. Tie in a bunch of hackle fibers on top of the hook extending over the thorax.

Step. 4.

Bend the remaining end of the wing case toward the bend of the hook. Fold the wing case forward dividing the bunch of hackle fibers and tie in at head.

Special Fly-Tying Instructions   **183**

SWANNUNDAZE STONE FLY NYMPH

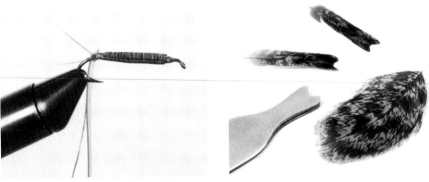

Step 1.

Wind lead wire half way down hook shank behind eye. Tie in two pieces of fly line on each side of lead wire extending to bend of hook. Dub a small ball of fur at the bend. Tie in 2 tails on the side of the hook divided by the ball of dubbing. Tie in a strand of ostrich herl and swannundaze. Before tying in swannundaze, taper the end for 3/16 inch.

Step 2.

To prepare wing cases, use a well marked feather such as ringneck pheasant body, speckled hen saddle or partridge. Shape 2 feathers with scissors or wing case burners then vinyl cement.

Step 3.

Spiral the swannundaze forward leaving a small space between each segment for the ostrich herl. The swannundaze should be ended halfway between the hook point and the eye. Wind ostrich herl forward. Dub a small amount of fur in front of the swannundaze and tie in legs on the side of body. Tie in wing case flat over back.

Step 4.

Dub a small amount of fur in front of the wing case. Tie in a second pair of legs and the second wing case. The excess portion of the second wing case should not be cut off since it will be used for the pronotum. Dub a small amount of fur in front of the second wing case and tie in third pair of legs. Tie in the pronotum at the head, tie off and lacquer.

See Page 194 for additional pattern descriptions.

Step 1.

Tie in body material and tinsel rib behind the eye and wrap thread to bend leaving a strand of tying thread 4 inches long extend past bend. Wrap tying thread to eye.

Step 2.

Wrap body material to eye allowing enough room to tie in hackle. Tie in 4 hen hackles at eye. Strip fibers from the bottom of the hackle to be tied to body.

Step 3.

Take two turns around the wing and hook with the tying thread that was left trailing from the bend. This operation will secure the wing to the hook. Spiral thread through the wing and tie in at eye. Spiral the tinsel forward, following the same path as the tying forward.

Step 4.

Tie in and wrap hackle collar style and tie off at eye.

MATUKA SCULPIN

Step 1.

Wind thread to bend of hook. Tie in tinsel rib and dub a tapered body. Tie in 4 speckled hen saddle feathers.

Step 2.

Wind tinsel rib through the wing toward the eye as described in the Matuka tying instructions in Volume I. Tie in 2 speckled hen saddle tips on the side of the body to form the pectoral fins.

Step 3.

Spin deer hair head and allow several strands to extend back to hook point. Clip head to shape.

Step 1.

Tie in tinsel body material at the eye and wrap to bend and return to the eye and tie off.

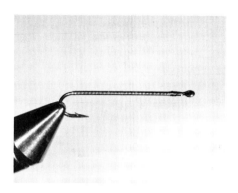

Step 2.

Tie in two sparse bunches of bucktail . . . light color on the belly and dark color on the back, facing forward. Tie off thread. Tie in red thread at the wing butts.

Step 3.

Pull the two bunches of bucktail toward the bend keeping them separated so that the belly and back fibers do not become intermingled. Secure the two bunches with the tying thread and tie off. Lacquer the head and paint on eyes.

TYING SINGLE EGG FLY

Step 1.

Start tying thread at the middle of the hook shank. Cut four pieces of yarn two inches long. If a spot of a different color is desired, cut a 2 inch strip of the second color. Place the pieces of yarn on top of the hook shank and take two or three wraps of tying thread around the bundle of yarn. Now pull hard to secure the bundle to the hook.

Step 2.

Grasp the ends of the yarn and pull upward. Take several wraps of tying thread in front and in back of the point where the yarn is bound to the hook.

Step 3.

Still holding the ends of the yarn, cut the yarn with a sharp pair of scissors or a razor blade at the point to give the desired egg diameter. Repeat these steps several times until you become proficient at the technique.

TYPICAL BASS HAIR BUG

Step 1.

Wind thread to bend of hook. Tie in 4 rubber legs on top of hook on top of which tie a whole maribou tip. Tie in 2 sadde hackles on each side, splayed outward.

Step 2.

Spin deer hair body and clip to desired shape. The deer hair should be packed as tight as possible to insure good flotation. Tie in 3 rubber legs on top of the hook with several figure 8 winds so that the legs extend 2 to 3 times the body width on each side of the hook.

Step 3.

Spin remainder of body and clip to desired shape. Tie off and lacquer head.

Step 1.

Wind thread to hook bend and tie in maribou. The maribou can be tied in any length or density to suit your needs. Wind thread to behind eye and dub body toward the hook bend.

Step 2.

Tie in a piece of acrylic yarn about 1/2 inch long across the hook shank using figure 8 winds. Tie in as many pieces as required to complete the body to the eye.

Step 3.

Tease out the acrylic yarn with a dubbing teaser, comb or wire brush until all the individual pieces appear to be blended into one.

Step 4.

Clip to shape. When completed, the body is flat and egg shaped.

Note: Bonefish flies should be tied inverted so the hook point rides up when fished. When tying a Giz Leech, the hook should be placed in the vise in the normal manner and the acrylic yarn tied in on top of the hook.

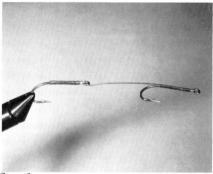

Step 1.

Attach nylon coated stainless wire to the trailing hook by placing wire through eye and securing the wire to the top of the hook shank with 4 layers of tying thread with a coating of lacquer between each layer. Cut the wire extending in front of the eye to 2½ inches. Secure the end of the wire to the lead hook using the same method as the trailing hook.

Step 2.

Cut a piece of medium mylar piping 5½ inches long. Slide mylar over the trailing hook and wire. Bend the wire until it follows the curve of the front hook. Slide the mylar over the front hook and stop when the mylar is on the shank. Pass the point through the mylar and allow the wire to straighten. Cut off excess mylar at head.

Step 3.

Tie in throat and wing at head. Cut and fray the mylar piping so it extends past the bend.

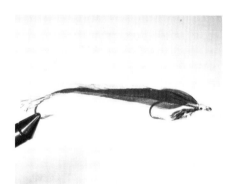

Step 4.

Tie in thread at bend to secure the mylar piping and wing.

Step 1.

The body is made from a 3 inch long by 1/2 inch diameter Cork Perch Float that may be purchased in your local tackle shop. Cut the float in half diagonally with a razor blade. Cut a slit in the corks, with a hacksaw blade, to accept the hook.

Step 2.

Bond the cork to the hook shank with either epoxy or hot glue.

Step 3.

Tie in either bucktail or saddle hackles extending 3 inches beyond the hook bend.

Step 4.

Coat cork with a good under-coating or primer before painting. Paint cork with a flexible enamel such as celluloid enamel to prevent chipping and cracking. Paint eyes.

ADDITIONAL DRY FLY PATTERNS

Cut Wing Thorax and Parachute Dries

Pattern	Blue Wing Olive	Pale Evening Dun	Hendrickson	Light Cahill
Tail/Hackle	Med. Dun	Light Dun	Bronze Dun	Dark Cream
Body	Olive	Primrose	Fawn Fox	Cream
Wing	Med. Dun	Light Dun	Med. Dun	Wood Duck

Delta/Elk/Chuck Wing Caddis

Pattern	Orange	Gray	Red Brown	Ginger
Body	Orange	Gray	Red Brown	Tan
Wing *	Cree	Med. Dun	Brown	Ginger
Hackle	Cree	Med. Dun	Brown	Ginger

* Hackle tip wing color for Delta Wing Caddis — Chuck and Elk Wing Caddis require Woodchuck and Elk hair respectively.

Waterwalkers

Pattern	Brown	Cream	Olive	Gray
Wing/Tail	Brown Elk	Light Tan Elk	Moose Body	Coastal Deer
Hackle	Brown	Cream	Dark Dun	Grizzly
Body	Brown Poly	Cream Poly	Olive Poly	Gray Poly

Hen Wing and Hackle Wing Spinners

Pattern	Rusty	Sulphur	Pale Olive	Trico
Wing *	Light Dun	Light Dun	Light Dun	White
Tail	Med. Dun	Light Dun	Light Dun	Light Dun
Body	Rusty Brown	Creamy Orange	Pale Olive	Black

* Neck hackle color for Hackle Wing Spinners or hen hackle tip color for Hen Wing Spinners.

Fur Extended Body Dries

Pattern	Brown Drake Spinner	Quill Gordon Thorax	Blue Wing Olive Dun
Underbody/ Tail	Tan Elk	Deer Dyed Med. Dun	Moose Body Hair
Body	Dirty Yellow Poly	Tan Poly	Medium Olive Poly
Wing	Lt. Dun Hen Tips or Poly	Dk. Dun Turkey Flat	Dk. Dun Hackle Tips
Hackle	None	Bronze Dun	Dark Dun

ADDITIONAL NYMPH PATTERNS

Tarchers

Pattern	Light	Medium	Dark	Rust
Tail	Wood Duck	Ringneck Pheasant Tail	Ringneck Pheasant Tail	Ringneck Pheasant Tail
Rib	Oval Gold	Oval Gold	Oval Gold	Oval Gold
Body *	Sand	Lt. Hare's Ear	Dk. Hare's Ear	Dark Rust
Wing Case	Speckled Hen Quill	Speckled Hen Quill	Speckled Hen Quill	Speckled Hen Quill
Legs	Wood Duck	Speckled Hen Body	Speckled Hen Body	Wood Duck

* Body and Head colors refer to Orvis Ultratranslucent Nymph Dubbing.

Translucent Caddis Pupa

Pattern	Cinnamon Sedge	Sand Sedge	Grannom	Brown Sedge
Body *	Dark Rust	Light Beige	Light Hare's Ear	Dark Hare's Ear
Legs	Natural Deer Hair and Wood Duck	Natural Deer Hair and Mallard	Natural Deer Hair and Mallard	Natural Deer Hair and Wood Duck
Pupal Wing	Gray Swiss Straw	Gray Swiss Straw	Gray Swiss Straw	Gray Swiss Straw
Head	Dark Hare's Ear	Light Hare's Ear	Dark Hare's Ear	Black Drake

* Body and Head colors refer to Orvis Ultratranslucent Nymph Dubbing.

Fur Caddis Pupa

Pattern	Sand Sedge	Speckled Sedge	Olive Sedge	Brown Sedge
Body	Pale Yellow	Light Brown	Pale Olive	Dark Brown
Pupal Wings	Mallard Quill	Mallard Quill	Mallard Quill	Mallard Quill
Legs & Head	Red Squirrel	Gray Squirrel	Red Squirrel	Gray Squirrel

Wiggle Nymphs

Pattern	March Brown	Light Cahill	Green Drake	Blue Wing Olive
Tail	Wood Duck	Wood Duck	Ringneck Pheasant Tail	Wood Duck
Body	Amber Fur	Creamy Tan Fur	Golden Olive Fur	Olive Fur
Rib	Brown Floss	None	Olive Floss	Brown Floss
Wing Case	Ringneck Pheasant Tail	Wood Duck	White Tip Turkey Tail	Canada Goose
Legs	Speckled Hen Body	Wood Duck	Wood Duck	Speckled Hen Body

Swannundaze Stone Flies

	Pattern	Giant Black	Early Brown	Little Yellow
	Tail	Canada Goose Quill	White Tip Turkey Tail	Amber Goose Quill
Style I	Abdomen *	Trans. Black	Dk. Trans. Amber	Lt. Trans. Amber
	Rib	Black Ostrich	Natural Gray Ostrich	Amber
Style II	Abdomen **	Black Drake	Lt. Hare's Ear	Yellow Stone
	Rib *	Trans. Black	Dk. Trans. Amber	Lt. Trans. Amber
	Thorax **	Black Drake	Lt. Hare's Ear	Yellow Stone
	Wing Cases	Dk. Speckled Hen Body	Speckled Hen Body	Ginger Hen Body
	Legs	Black Hen Hackle	Speckled Hen Body	Ginger Hen Hackle

* Colors refer to Standard Swannundaze.
** Colors refer to Orvis Ultratranslucent Nymph Dubbing.